Green Kitchen
at Home

David Frenkiel
and Luise Vindahl

Green Kitchen
at Home

Quick and healthy vegetarian
food for every day

hardie grant books

To Elsa, Isac and baby Gabriel

Contents

Introduction

We have a confession to make. And a promise.

First, the confession. Whenever we write '*We love this recipe*', it doesn't automatically mean that it is something that we continue to cook at home. As food and recipe development is our job, we are constantly trying new methods, flavours and ingredient combinations. So, even if a recipe is delicious and a real favourite on the very week we are publishing it (online, in a magazine or in a book), it isn't always cut out for our family's needs and habits (or our children's preferences).

And now the promise. This book is filled with the recipes that we actually make most often in our kitchen. Our true favourites. We have been cooking many of these repeatedly during the last few years and know them by heart.

Since we are a family of four (five, when this book is printed), there are lots of quick, simple and child-friendly vegetarian dishes that we turn to during stressful weekdays. And also slightly more elaborate dishes that we often make at the weekend when we have friends or family coming over. Most of our daily breakfasts are included and also the simple desserts that can be tossed together while the kids are watching a cartoon. Recipes that are fun to make, taste great and strike the right balance between interesting and uncomplicated. But more than just recipes, we wanted this book to be a demonstration of how we build our meals at home, the shortcuts we take and the tricks we have learnt in the kitchen. Cooking real food every day can be challenging for any working person or family, so we are sharing our best ways to eat well even when the fridge is half-empty and our kids are banging the table, chanting that they are hungry.

Our food

Food for us is basically all about feeling good. The process of cooking, the pleasure of eating and the energy we get from it. They all serve the same joyful purpose. Few things are as important and meaningful as the ceremony around food, and many of our best memories are connected with it – from the smell of cinnamon in the Marrakech Medina to hilarious moments with the kids around our kitchen table. I can't for the life of me remember the plot of the last movie we watched but I will forever remember the way our daughter always closed her eyes, tilted her head back and said '*mmmmmm*' after each bite of food when she was a toddler.

Our recipes are deeply focused around vegetables, but also feature wholegrains, good fats, natural sweeteners, nuts, seeds, legumes and fruit. We have developed our unique way of cooking through years of living together. I have been a vegetarian for more than 20 years and have learnt to handle myself decently in a kitchen through experience. Luise has always been a naturally talented cook, but has also studied nutritional therapy to gain a further understanding about the importance of food for overall health. We don't always get along in the kitchen, but it feels like we complement each other. I would probably indulge too much and too often without her and she might get a little too focused on nutritional values without me. And as the kids have become part of our kitchen, they have slowly but steadily wiped away all snobbish methods or ingredients that we might previously have been drawn to.

When we talk about our food as healthy, we don't mean it in a restricting, 'you can't eat this or that' type of way. For us, health is solely about wellbeing and that includes the bubbling excitement that comes from indulging in the occasional butter- and sugar-heavy Swedish cardamom bun from the sourdough bakery across the street.

I think it's safe to say that most people will feel great as a result of cooking the recipes in this book, but health is very individual. My body reacts differently to food from Luise's. We crave different types of food, preparation methods and ingredients depending on if we are spending a winter in northern Sweden or a summer in Italy, if we are doing a lot of physical activity or sitting still in an office, or, as now, if Luise is pregnant or not. There isn't one way of eating that is good for everyone. We need to listen to our bodies and try to find a way of eating that makes us feel good. And also find a level of cooking that feels doable.

We don't put labels on what we eat, so even if most flours in our store cupboard happen to be gluten-free and many recipes are suitable for vegans, we do eat eggs and would choose a sourdough wholegrain bread with only 3 ingredients over a gluten-free toast with 15 refined ingredients.

As far as we can, we focus on seasonal ingredients. It's a simple way to get a natural variation in our diet throughout the year. Vegetables in season also taste better, are cheaper and more sustainable and thus better for our environment.

At home

It feels like Luise and I have talked a thousand times (in books, magazine interviews and online) about how our journey started in Rome, almost 10 years ago. How our different approaches to food (I was the unhealthy vegetarian and she was the healthy carnivore) led us to a new way of cooking and eating together. But what we rarely talk about is that we are constantly evolving, as individuals and as a family. And the way we cook and eat is reflected by those changes.

When we wrote our first cookbook, our daughter Elsa was just a toddler and our only child, which meant that one of us could always find time to cook. She also ate basically anything we put in front of her. As I am writing this, we are only weeks away from having our third child. Elsa has just started school and our two-year-old son, Isac, is a tornado of energy who climbs chairs, ovens and tables and thinks our phones are the perfect indoor ice skates. He is obsessed with fruit and roasted vegetables but not as obsessed with leafy vegetables or anything with the wrong consistency.

Because our lives at home have become more stressful, time is now an important factor in our cooking. You will see how that is reflected in this book both by the prep and time estimates, but also by the fact that many of the recipes are really quick. Versatility is another factor that we have considered. With more people in our family there are also more opinions. A lot of our dinners are spent listening to our daughter explaining how she loves this [*pointing at oven-roasted broccoli*] and hates that [*holds up a mushroom between two fingers like it was poison*], loves this [*places three raw carrots in her mouth at the same time*] and hates that

[*scoops the lettuce off her plate and onto her little brother's*]. The difficult part is that she can be quite random about it, devouring avocado-on-toast one day and then the next day saying, 'I have ALWAYS hated avocado, you know that!' So, even if we don't let the kids dictate the dinner entirely, we have become quite experienced in creating meals that are versatile and adaptable so they can always find things that they like. Therefore we are sharing ideas on how to vary ingredients to preference or season in almost every recipe in this book. Even if we refer to our children, this book is not solely for families. We believe most people today are looking for quick, healthy and smart vegetarian recipes that everyone can enjoy – kids and adults alike.

The first chapter is called Fridge Favourites and it is probably the most important. The staples in that chapter are our building blocks for lots of recipes in the book and, when time is short, we also simply combine them with each other for quick and fuss-free meals.

The other chapters are pretty straightforward. We have simply divided them into Breakfast, Handy Meals, During the Week, At the Weekend, Spreads and Sides and Desserts to make it as easy as possible to find the right recipe for your current situation.

There are quite a few recipes in this book that have almost become a trademark of our family – like the Spinach Crêpes that we stuff with creamy chickpeas (garbanzo beans), apple, tahini and mushrooms (page 127), the Baked Carrot Cake Oatmeal (page 56) that we often make for weekend breakfasts and the Middle-Eastern Cauliflower and Lentil Salad (page 184) that we make at least a couple of times every month. They started out as posts on our blog and we have been perfecting them over the years.

But there are also loads of previously unpublished recipes that we are really thrilled to introduce. You have to try our unusual take on fish and chips (page 157), using leek, courgette (zucchini) and cauliflower to make the no-fish cakes. And the Broccoli, Spinach and Apple Muffins (page 89) that our kids are often munching on. As well as the Mediterranean Tray-bake with Halloumi Chunks (page 116) that has become a new weeknight standard in our home, we have included a bunch of hearty salads in the book that are perfect for dinner rather than as sides. And there's a selection of fuss-free soups. We have put extra focus on comforting dishes, too, such as pasta recipes (pages 92, 115 and 144), Flatbread Pizzette (page 133) and waffle toasties (page 140).

All the dishes are easy to make and easy to like and all have been tested – not only by the jury of our two children, as well as our assistant – but also by a separate tester in a New Zealand kitchen, on the other side of the world from us, to make sure the recipes work and taste good, regardless of where you live.

It almost feels like a gift, passing these recipes on to you, and we hope dearly that they will become as popular in your kitchen as they are in ours. *David*

How to use this book

Our style of cooking isn't built on exactitude. Every meal involves a certain degree of improvisation. Whenever we have half a vegetable in the fridge, it goes into whatever is cooking on the stove. And before serving, we always taste and adjust the flavours one last time to get the right balance – salt, pepper, fresh herbs, a squeeze of lemon, maybe a dollop of yoghurt on top – a lot happens to the dish just before it goes on the plate.

Regardless of how detailed our recipes are, they will not be the same dish in your kitchen. Vegetables vary in size, flavour and texture depending on season, ripeness and where they have been growing. A roasted pumpkin might need 30 minutes in our oven and 40 minutes in yours, and your variety of potatoes might be more thick-skinned than ours. We have tried to make these recipes as easy and yet instructive as possible, but we do ask that you taste and season dishes before you serve them, check the texture of your baked goods before removing them from the oven and take liberties to substitute an ingredient if it's not in season or is unavailable where you live. We also recommend that you read the full recipe before you get started in the kitchen.

Time

All recipes have rough time estimates. The actual time, of course, varies from person to person, depending on how quick you are with the knife or whether you cook water on a gas hob or an old electric one, but these estimates will at least give you an indication of whether this is a quick, medium or more time-consuming recipe. If we refer to a Fridge Favourite in a recipe, the time estimate doesn't include the time it takes to make that staple, since we encourage you to keep these on hand.

Gluten-free alternatives

We recommend adapting our recipes to your specific needs. So for a strictly gluten-free alternative to our recipes using oats, choose certified gluten-free oats or another gluten-free rolled grain.

Measurements

Since we are lucky enough to have our books published in a number of countries all over the world we have tried to provide measurements and amounts that will work regardless of whether you live in Melbourne, London or Seattle. Following weights will always give you the most exact result. But if you measure flour in volume, know that a cup should always be full but not packed. A handful of herbs or spinach is roughly 30 g (1 oz).

1 cup = 250 ml
⅓ cup = 80 ml
¼ cup = 60 ml
1 tbsp = 15 ml
1 tsp = 5 ml

Tools

We just wanted to briefly mention a few special tools and pieces of equipment that are especially handy in a kitchen focused around vegetables. These are a constant help in our kitchen when we're preparing vegetables. We are not mentioning the obvious knife, frying pan (skillet) and saucepan here, but a good set of those is of course also essential.

Spiralizer or julienne peeler
A spiralizer is a great tool for transforming vegetables into fun ribbons. We add them to salads or use them instead of spaghetti. Our kids prefer real spaghetti over courgetti but they love carrot or cucumber noodles/strips in a salad.

Our spiralizer is on the top shelf in our kitchen so most days we just use the julienne peeler that lives in our kitchen drawer.

Mandoline
Although dangerous for fingertips, a mandoline is really useful for shaving thin strips of raw vegetables. It can make any salad pretty and it is also more pleasant to eat thinly shaved vegetables than large, thick chunks. Fennel, carrots, beetroot, radish and cauliflower all turn out amazing when thinly shaved.

Steaming basket
We use a simple bamboo basket to steam broccoli, asparagus, string beans, or simply when heating up something from the freezer. We usually just place it on top of a pot of pasta or potatoes that's cooking and it's honestly no hassle at all.

Blender

This is our most trusted tool. We use our blender to whiz up smoothies daily, but also for making vegetable-flavoured crêpe batter, blending soups or smoothie bowls. After a long run with cheaper blenders, we upgraded to a high-end, high-speed blender (Vitamix). It is pricey but we have been using it a lot since we got it, and we also tend to blend more varieties of vegetables than we used to since they can be mixed completely smooth.

Scale

Weighing ingredients is always more exact than measuring them in a cup, so if you want to make sure you get the right amount, an electric scale is helpful.

A food processor or immersion (hand) blender

We use our food processor for making pesto, hummus, nut butter, raw desserts and whenever we are shredding large amounts of cabbage and vegetables.

We used to own an immersion (hand) blender with a food processor bowl add-on. It worked perfectly in our small kitchen but unfortunately couldn't keep up with the amount of food we mixed, and eventually broke down. Now we have a Magimix high-end food processor with a wide base and induction motor, which means that it doesn't get overheated. It makes amazingly smooth hummus and nut butter, but also takes up more space and is quite costly. In a small kitchen, an immersion blender goes a long way.

Muffin tin

This is perhaps a rather odd piece of equipment to recommend, but we use our muffin tin on a weekly basis. It is of course essential for making muffins – both savoury (page 89) and sweet (page 52) – but we also use it for frittata (page 103), making portion-sized baked oatmeal and for making hand-size versions of our Spinach and Feta Quiche (page 105).

Shopping List

In our first book, we presented a store cupboard list that was so extensive that even we got tired of reading it. We are keeping it simpler here. Instead of explaining every single ingredient in our kitchen, we have just focused on the ones that we use all the time and organised them into a shopping list. Our hope is that this can be a concrete guideline if you are trying to change your cooking habits and need help prioritising the essentials amid the jungle of ingredients at the grocery store. With this list on hand, you will be set up for most recipes in this book.

ON THE COUNTER

Apple cider vinegar
Black pepper
Coconut oil
Fresh herbs
Fruit (a selection of seasonal
    varieties)
Honey
Maple syrup
Olive oil
Rye bread
Sea salt

DRY GOODS

Almonds
Almond flour (or almond meal)
Arrowroot/potato starch/corn starch
Buckwheat flour
Buckwheat groats
Cashew nuts
Coconut milk
Dried apricots
Flaxseeds
Hazelnuts
Lentils (a selection of colours)
Millet
Organic vegetable stock cubes
Pumpkin seeds
Quinoa
Raisins
Rice flour
Rolled oats
Soft dates
Sunflower seeds
Tinned beans (a selection of varieties)
Tinned tomatoes (whole and crushed)
Wholegrain pasta or bean pasta
    (a selection of varieties)
Wholegrain rice

DRIED SPICES

Cardamom
Cayenne
Cinnamon
Cumin
Curry
Ginger
Sumac or za'atar
Turmeric

FRIDGE

Almond milk (or other plant-based
    milks)
Butter (dairy and nut)
Eggs
Feta
Oat milk
Tahini
Tofu
Vegetables (a selection of seasonal
    varieties)
Yoghurt (dairy or plant-based)

FREEZER

Bananas
Berries (a selection of varieties)
Broccoli
Peas
Spinach

Fridge Favourites

This is the story of how a pot of cooked quinoa, a jar of lentils and two trays of roasted roots became a dinner salad on a Tuesday, a soup topping on a Wednesday and part of a lunch frittata on a Friday.

Most people can pull together a well-balanced, veg-based meal with the right time, recipe and ingredients on hand. But if you take away time, things tend to get tricky. The whole idea of cooking something that tastes good and is good for you in under 20 minutes can feel daunting if you haven't planned ahead. Especially if you also happen to have a cranky child/husband/wife/roommate in the house. When stress levels are high, our inspiration always seem to vanish and heading to the Thai restaurant around the corner becomes a much easier option.

These fridge staples are our way of handling that. We see them as shortcuts to proper meals. Fast food, almost. And we always try to have them on standby, in the fridge, ready to choose from. On their own, these basic recipes are quick and easy to prepare; by having them readily available in the fridge, we make dinner preparation one step shorter, which is usually exactly what we need to start cooking during the week. Many of them can also be bought pre-made in the supermarket. Homemade of course tastes best, and it is the healthiest and cheapest option, but for days when we haven't had time to mix up a hummus or pesto, store-bought is a good shortcut. Just choose the option with the shortest or most natural ingredient list.

On the following pages, we turn these staples into different meals, but by simply pairing them with each other and adding one extra ingredient, you have a whole array of simple dishes. Here are a few suggestions:

Quick Quinoa + *Perfect Pesto* + *cherry tomatoes* = Simple salad
Lazy Lentils + *Heavenly Hummus* + *Roasted Roots* + *chopped apple* = Hearty lunch
Big Batch Tomato Sauce + *Quick Quinoa* + *egg* = Satisfying dinner
Rice Crêpes + *Heavenly Hummus* + *Lazy Lentils* = Filled crêpes
Rainbow Flatbreads + *Pumpkin Purée* + *Perfect Pesto* = Quick toast or pizza
Big-batch Tomato Sauce + *Lazy Lentils* + *spaghetti* = Easy dinner for the kids

We've also included a chia pudding in this chapter, as it is something we keep for quick breakfasts, snacks or desserts. *David & Luise*

Big-batch Tomato Sauce

Makes 2.25 litres (9 cups)

Prep + cook time:
45 minutes

With a good tomato sauce bottled in the fridge you are only minutes away from countless delicious and wholesome meals. We've included this recipe because we'd like to encourage you to make huge batches so you always have it available. Another good thing about making big batches of sauce is that the flavours keep on developing, so it always tastes better on days 2 and 3.

If you are making a specific meal that requires a tomato sauce (in this book or another), make a habit of doubling the amount of sauce, and bottle the leftovers.

We always give our sauce plenty of time to reduce on the stove, as this transforms the tartness in the tomatoes into sweet tones. We also add the basil stems together with the onion as the stem carries a lot of flavour. You can add extra spices and vegetables to the sauce, but we keep ours simple and instead add flavours when we use it for specific recipes.

Check out the Family-style Tortilla Bowls (page 179), Shakshuka (page 148), Popeye Polpette (page 171), Lemon Ricotta Lasagne for a Crowd (page 182) and Flatbread Pizzette (page 133) for various ways to use this sauce.

4 tbsp extra-virgin olive oil
3 onions, peeled
6 cloves of garlic, peeled
50 g (1¾ oz/1 cup) fresh basil
4 tbsp capers, drained and rinsed (optional)

4 tbsp tomato purée (paste)
6 × 400 g (14 oz) tins chopped tomatoes
sea salt and freshly ground black pepper

Heat the oil in your largest saucepan on a medium-low heat. Finely chop the onions, garlic and basil stems, transfer to the pan and sauté for about 10 minutes, or until the onions have softened. Add the capers (if using), tomato purée and tinned tomatoes and season to taste with salt and pepper. Bring to the boil, reduce the heat and simmer for at least 30 minutes or until the sauce is flavoursome and has reduced, stirring from time to time so as not to burn the base. Add more water to loosen the sauce if it becomes too dry.

Remove from the heat, stir through the basil leaves, cover and set aside to cool and for the flavours to enhance. Store the sauce in the fridge in sealable glass bottles and it will keep for at least 4–5 days. Alternatively, freeze it in freezer bags or containers.

Perfect Pesto

Makes 220 g
(7¾ oz/1 cup)

Prep + cook time:
10 minutes

TIPS:
For a vegan alternative, replace the cheese with 50 g (1¾ oz/ ⅓ cup) cashew nuts and 2 tbsp nutritional yeast flakes.

For a nut-free alternative, replace the pine nuts with pumpkin seeds or sunflower seeds.

The pesto can also be prepared in a medium-sized bowl with an immersion (hand) blender or by using a mortar and pestle.

For us, pesto is more than just a dressing for pasta. It's a shortcut flavouring option for numerous meals. It can be used on top of a flatbread pizza instead of tomato sauce (page 133), mashed with avocado to add flavour and creaminess to a pasta salad (page 92), used as a flavour boost on top of frittata muffins (page 103) or whisked up with oil and lemon to make a salad dressing (page 87).

This is our standard, basic pesto recipe, just like Luise's Italian nonna makes it. You can use a store-bought option, of course, but homemade always tastes better.

We also make a vegan version with nutritional yeast and cashew nuts to keep it creamy instead of the cheese (see tips). The nutritional yeast adds that cheesy flavour, making the two versions very similar.

If you feel like playing around with this recipe, you can add kale, spinach, rocket or even raw broccoli to the herbs. The pine nuts can be substituted with other nuts, and you can even try adding sweet fruit, like mango or raisins, for an interesting flavour twist.

100 g (3½ oz/4 cups) fresh basil, leaves and stems picked
60 g (2 oz/⅔ cup) Grana Padano or Parmigiano Reggiano, grated
50 g (1¾ oz/⅓ cup) pine nuts, toasted

80 ml (2½ fl oz/⅓ cup) extra-virgin olive oil
2 tbsp lemon juice
1 clove of garlic, peeled
sea salt and freshly ground black pepper

Place all of the ingredients in a food processor or blender, season to taste with salt and pepper and blend until well combined.

Store the pesto in the fridge in a sealable glass jar and it will keep for about a week. Alternatively, roll it into a log using a sheet of parchment paper and store it in the freezer.

Heavenly Hummus

Makes 675 g
(1½ lb/3 cups)

Prep + cook time:
(full version) 2 hours
+ 24 hours soaking
(quick version)
10 minutes

With hummus, you have three options: you either make the full version from scratch using dried chickpeas, make a quick version using tinned cooked chickpeas, or you simply head to the closest supermarket and buy the hummus with the shortest ingredient list. In all honesty, we go for all of these options, depending on the day and situation. Our golden rule, however, is always to keep a jar of hummus at home – it's such a versatile and tasty spread.

It features in a few of our recipes in this book: underneath a Shakshuka (page 148), on top of our #GKS Bowl (page 111), and inside our breakfast Flatbread Sandwiches (page 71). We're sharing two versions here, but if you'd rather go for option no. 3, we've got your back on that as well.

200 g (7 oz/1 cup) dried chickpeas
  (garbanzo beans)
½ tsp bicarbonate of soda
  (baking soda)
1 tsp sea salt
2 cloves of garlic, peeled

120 ml (4 fl oz/½ cup) hulled tahini
juice of 1 lemon
2 tbsp extra-virgin olive oil
½ tsp ground cumin
sea salt, to taste

FULL VERSION: Place the chickpeas and bicarbonate of soda in a medium-sized bowl, cover with 600 ml (20 fl/2½ cups) of water and mix until combined. Soak in the fridge or 24 hours.

Drain and rinse the chickpeas and transfer them to a medium-sized saucepan along with the salt, 2 litres (8 cups) of water and garlic. Bring to the boil, then reduce the heat and simmer for 1–2 hours or until the chickpeas are tender, skimming off any foam. Drain, reserving 120 ml (4 fl oz/½ cup) of the cooking water, and set aside to cool.

Place the chickpeas, garlic, reserved cooking water and remaining ingredients in a food processor or blender and pulse until completely smooth.

Store in the fridge in a sealable glass jar. It will keep for up to 1 week.

QUICK VERSION: Drain and rinse 2 × 400 g (14 oz) tins chickpeas (garbanzo beans). Place them with ½ cup of hot water and the same quantities as the full version of garlic, tahini, lemon juice, oil and cumin, in a food processor or blender, season to taste with salt and blend until completely smooth.

Store in the fridge in a sealable glass jar. It will keep for up to 1 week.

TIPS:
Alternatively, prepare the hummus in a medium-sized bowl with an immersion blender.

Try adding 1 raw grated beetroot to your mixture for a pink and slightly sweet hummus. Or 1 tbsp ground turmeric and some freshly ground black pepper for a tasty yellow option. You can also replace the chickpeas with white beans.

Pumpkin Purée

Makes approx. 1 kg
(2.2 lb/4 cups)

Prep + cook time:
50 minutes

Pumpkin's rich, slightly sweet and very creamy flesh is great on top of a sandwich (page 177), in smoothies, as a soup (page 137), in a quiche, in sweet dishes (page 243) and – of course – in the classic American dessert, pumpkin pie. In some countries you can buy tinned pumpkin purée, but making it yourself is a breeze.

We use the term pumpkin here also for butternut squash. Even if it is technically regarded as a winter squash, it is a pumpkin all the same.

1.8 kg (4 lb) butternut squash,
    pumpkin or winter squash of
    choice
1 tbsp virgin coconut oil, melted
1 tsp sea salt

Preheat the oven to 200°C (400°F/Gas mark 6) and line a baking tray with parchment paper.

Cut the squash in half lengthwise, rub the oil over the flesh, sprinkle with the salt and place on the tray, cut sides face down. Bake for about 45 minutes or until the flesh is tender and the skin is golden and blistered.

Remove from the oven and set aside to cool slightly before discarding the seeds and fibrous strings and scooping out the soft flesh into a large bowl. Using a fork, mash the flesh, transfer to a sieve to drain any excess liquid, then set aside to cool completely.

Store the purée in the fridge in an airtight container and it will keep for about a week. Alternatively, freeze it.

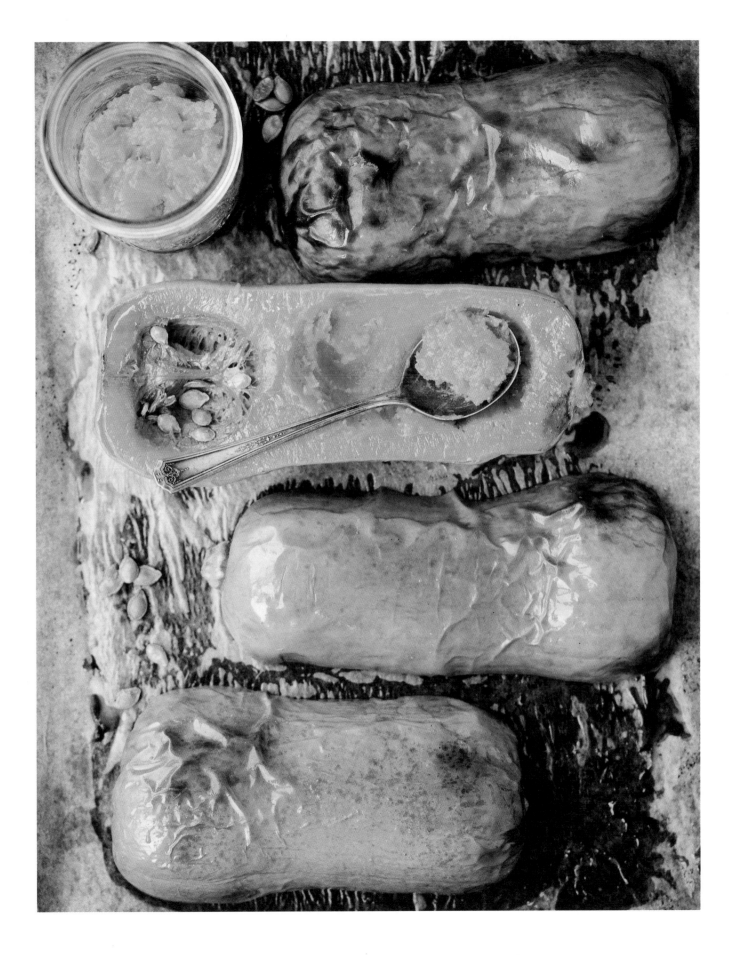

Quick Quinoa

Makes 900 g (2 lb/6 cups)

Prep + cook time:
20 minutes

We acknowledge that cooking quinoa hardly calls for a recipe, as all you need to do is follow the instructions on the packet. However, we have included it in this chapter to point out how helpful it is always to have cooked quinoa ready and available in the fridge. We constantly add it to salads (page 123), use it with sauces instead of rice or pasta, in stir-fries (page 130) and as a filler in polpette (page 171). So, next time you cook quinoa, empty the whole packet into the saucepan and store the cooked leftovers in glass jars in the fridge. Then go ahead and try some of the quinoa recipes in this book throughout the week. You will thank us later.

400 g (14 oz/2 cups) quinoa, colour
   of choice, rinsed
1 litre (32 fl oz/4 cups) water
1 tsp sea salt

TIP:
You can add flavour to the quinoa by cooking it with spices (cinnamon sticks, cardamom pods etc.) or by replacing half of the water with vegetable stock.

Place the quinoa, water and salt in a large saucepan, cover and bring to the boil, then reduce the heat and simmer for 15–18 minutes or until small tails are visible on the seeds and the water is absorbed. Remove from the heat, fluff up with a fork and set aside to cool.

Store the quinoa in the fridge in an airtight container and it will keep for about a week. Alternatively, freeze it.

Rice Crêpe Batter

Makes approx. 12 crêpes

Prep + cook time:
10 minutes + 30 minutes
rest time + frying time

This crêpe batter is one of our family's most cherished recipes. It can be used for basic crêpes or thin pancakes, but we often add vegetables to make it more interesting and it is also a really great way to sneak greens into your kids' diet.

In this book, we add spinach and serve them with a chickpea and apple filling (page 127), we add carrots and roll them into Korean Carrot Crêpe Rolls (page 97) and we add beetroot and eat them as dessert crêpes (page 219). This gluten-free batter is heavy on egg and is made with rice flour, which makes the crêpes unusually easy to flip and handle, even more so when the batter has rested in the fridge. We often make a double batch of batter, saving half of it in a sealed jar in the fridge. It feels like such a luxury to have a batter ready to go, for any breakfast, lunch or speedy-dinner situation. Just remember to whisk it before using.

5 free-range eggs
500 ml (16 fl oz/2 cups) plant-based
    milk of choice (e.g. oat milk)
150 g (5¼ oz/1 cup) rice flour

1 tbsp butter or virgin coconut oil,
    melted, plus extra to fry
1 tsp sea salt

Crack the eggs into a blender or food processor, add the rest of the ingredients, blend until completely smooth, pour into a jug and set aside in the fridge for about 30 minutes to rest. (You can leave it for up to 3 days.)

Heat a little butter or oil in a 20 cm (8 inch) non-stick frying pan (skillet) on a medium-high heat. Once hot, whisk the batter then ladle 80 ml (2½ fl oz/⅓ cup) into the pan, tilting the pan to spread and evenly distribute the batter. Fry for 1–2 minutes or until small bubbles form on the surface and the base is golden. Run a spatula around the edges of the crêpe, to make sure it has detached from the pan, before carefully flipping it over and frying the other side for a further 1–2 minutes or until cooked and golden. Transfer to a plate and repeat with the rest of the batter (you may need to reduce the heat slightly after the first crêpe).

TIP:
Alternatively, prepare the crêpe batter in a large mixing bowl with a whisk or immersion (hand) blender.

Roasted Roots and Veg

Makes 1 kg (2.2 lb/8 cups)

Prep + cook time:
40 minutes

Roasted vegetables truly are one of the easiest dishes we cook at home. Often we prepare the vegetables for specific meals, but on weekends we also fill large trays with a mix of roots and vegetables that we roast and add to meals throughout the week. It's not a precise process: we just chop roots and vegetables, tip them onto trays, drizzle with oil and salt, roast and then store in glass containers in the fridge.

We always tuck roasted roots in our #GKS Bowls (page 111) but they are also amazing inside a Rye Waffle Toastie (page 140), in our Roasted Root and Frittata Muffins (page 103), with pasta or a salad.

Even though roots are essential, we often add another vegetable (like broccoli, fennel or cauliflower) for a more versatile mix. Other roots and vegetables that can be used are parsley root, beetroot (beet), butternut squash and celeriac root.

To vary the flavouring, try a sprinkling of cinnamon for a Christmas twist, sumac, lemon and chilli for a Middle Eastern version, and rosemary and thyme for a Mediterranean flavour.

1.8 kg (4 lb) mixed roots and vegetables, trimmed, tops and seeds removed and peeled where applicable (e.g. sweet potato, potato, carrot, parsnip, broccoli head and stalk

4 tbsp extra-virgin olive oil
sea salt and freshly ground black pepper

Preheat the oven to 200°C (400°F/Gas mark 6) and line two baking trays with parchment paper.

Cut the root vegetables and trimmed broccoli stalks into bite-sized pieces and the broccoli into small florets. Spread the root vegetables and broccoli stems out on the trays, and set aside the broccoli florets. Drizzle the oil over the vegetables, season to taste with salt and pepper and toss until well coated. Bake for 25–30 minutes or until the vegetables are tender and golden, adding the broccoli florets 10 minutes through the cooking time.

Remove from the oven and set aside to cool completely. Store the vegetables in the fridge in an airtight container and they will keep for about a week.

Lazy Lentils

We tend to cook double or triple portions of lentils, just like with quinoa, rice and other grains and pseudo-grains, and store them in glass jars in the fridge so we always have a healthy protein source quickly available. Lentils have that magical ability to turn any light side dish into a proper meal. Topping a soup with lentils and chopped pumpkin seeds always makes it more filling (page 146), they add sustenance to any salad (page 184) and body to burgers (page 187).

Black lentils are our favourite for this type of recipe as they stay intact and can be stored without going mushy, but green or brown also work well. Red and yellow lentils are more appropriate for soups and stews.

Makes 800 g
(1¾ lb/4 cups)

Prep + Cook time:
25 minutes

400 g (14 oz/2 cups) beluga, puy
    or green lentils, rinsed
1.5 litres (6 cups) water
1 tsp salt

Place the lentils and 1.5 litres (6 cups) of water in a large saucepan, cover and bring to the boil, then reduce the heat and simmer for 20–25 minutes or until the lentils are tender. Stir in the salt towards the end of the cooking time. Drain and set aside to cool.

Store the lentils in the fridge in an airtight container and they will keep for up to 1 week. Alternatively, freeze them.

TIP:
You can flavour the lentils by adding a few bay leaves during cooking. Or cook them in vegetable stock.

Rainbow Flatbreads

Makes 12–16 slices

Prep + cook time:
40 minutes

Here is a great example of how to get vegetables into all kinds of food. In these flatbreads, vegetables are actually the main ingredient (which is why they have such fantastic colours). If you don't count the herbs, this recipe only has three ingredients and they can be used as a base for many dishes. In this book, we use them to make sandwiches (page 71) and pizza (page 133). Another trick is to create cute little canapés (using cookie cutters) with various toppings for a buffet table. We make the green broccoli bread most often at home and have therefore focused on that recipe, but we've also included instructions for how to make versions with carrots and beetroot (see tip).

1 large broccoli (500 g/1 lb), head and stalk (or 2 small)
100 g (3½ oz/1 cup) almond flour

1 tsp dried herbs of choice (e.g. oregano, thyme or basil)
sea salt and freshly ground black pepper
4 free-range eggs

Preheat the oven to 200°C (400°F/Gas mark 6) and line a baking tray with parchment paper.

Roughly chop the broccoli, place it in a food processor and blend until the texture resembles breadcrumbs. Measure out 400 g (14 oz/4 cups) of the vegetable 'breadcrumbs'. Transfer them to a medium-sized mixing bowl, add the rest of the dry ingredients, season to taste with salt and pepper, mix until combined and make a well in the centre.

Crack the eggs into the well. Using a fork, whisk the eggs before gradually incorporating the dry ingredients. Work the loose 'dough', using your hands, until it comes together and then shape it into a ball. Transfer to the lined baking tray and, using your hands, flatten the dough into a rectangle about 7.5 mm (⅓ inch) thick.

Transfer the tray to the oven and bake for about 25 minutes, or until slightly golden and firm. Remove from the oven and set aside to cool completely before turning upside down to carefully remove the parchment paper. Cut into roughly 10 × 4 cm (4 × 1½ inch) slices.

Store the flatbreads in the fridge in an airtight container and they will keep for a few days.

TIP:
To make beetroot (beet) flatbread, replace the broccoli with equal amounts of cauliflower and grated beetroot. To make carrot flatbread, replace the broccoli with equal amounts of cauliflower and grated carrot. For both recipes, follow the instructions for the broccoli flatbread.

Chia to Share

Makes approx. 500 ml
(16 fl oz/2 cups)

Prep + cook time:
5 minutes + 20 minutes
soaking

With a jar of chia pudding ready in the fridge, you have a number of delicious options when energy levels are running low and you are in need of a quick treat.

A bowl of chia pudding with any fresh seasonal fruit, a drop of honey or maple syrup for sweetness, a dollop of nut butter and a splash of milk is always a good option. Or try serving it in a jar with a creamy raspberry mousse on top (page 46). Another equally quick but a tad more indulgent option is to layer it with quick-stewed seasonal fruit, nuts, seeds and yoghurt in a glass as a weeknight dessert (page 231).

We prefer our chia pudding creamy but not too thick, and have found this ratio to be perfect. It can also be nice to add lime or lemon zest for a bit of tanginess.

> 6 tbsp chia seeds (colour
>   of choice)
> ½ tsp ground vanilla or
>   1 tsp vanilla extract
> 500 ml (16 fl oz/2 cups) plant-based
>   milk of choice

Place all of the ingredients in a medium-sized mixing bowl and whisk until combined.

Whisk from time to time in the first 10 minutes to prevent any lumps from forming, then set aside to soak in the fridge for at least 20 minutes until thick and jelly-like (or leave overnight).

Store the chia pudding in the fridge in a sealable glass jar and it will keep for a few days.

Breakfast

My grandfather was a farmer. Every morning he would get up at 5 a.m. to feed the animals and do all the farm duties. After he was done with his first shift, he would go into the kitchen to cook oatmeal or porridge. Around then I would wake up. I don't know what his secret was but his oatmeal always had that perfect, thick and creamy consistency without losing the oaty texture. I was only a child but have such strong memories of him standing by the stove with his back facing the kitchen table and the sound of a wooden spoon stirring against the bottom of the pot.

I have become my grandpa. I don't get up at 5 a.m. and we don't have any cows and horses to feed, but porridge is also a morning ritual in our home. Everyone in our family loves eating it and I love to make it – stirring the pot, pretending that I'm him. We are sharing three variations of oatmeal in this chapter, but also some contemporary versions of porridge – a baked variety with carrots and raisins, a cold overnight porridge with buckwheat and blueberries, and a creamy, grain-free quinoa and millet porridge with turmeric and warm spices.

On days when we don't cook porridge, we often choose a dish that involves eggs, like the Full Vegetarian Breakfast (page 44), a herby quinoa bowl (page 50) or our Banana and Spinach Pancakes (page 54). A few other common breakfasts in our house that we have included in this chapter are simple rye slices with a variety of toppings (page 59), Fruit-flavoured Yoghurt Pots (page 76), Banana and Cacao Granola (page 75) and our epic Turmeric and Blueberry Breakfast Muffins (page 52).

There is a mix of sweet and savoury breakfasts in this chapter so hopefully you'll find a few new favourites of your own. *David*

Full Vegetarian Breakfast

Serves 2

Prep + cook time:
25 minutes

We make this slightly modernised, vegetarian interpretation of a 'Full English Breakfast' whenever we crave something savoury in the morning. It's warm, filling and generous without being too heavy, like the traditional version often is. Apple and kale keeps the flavours interesting, while browned onions, mushrooms, sweet potatoes and Brussels sprouts make it rich and hearty. We love to add some sriracha or gochujang sauce for a sweet and spicy flavour punch, but regular chilli sauce or even a good-quality ketchup can be used instead. The servings are quite generous here, so if you are a small family, it should still be enough for all of you with the addition of one or two extra eggs.

2 tbsp extra-virgin olive oil
1 onion, peeled
½ sweet potato, peeled
10 Brussels sprouts, trimmed
10 mushrooms of choice, cleaned
10 cherry tomatoes
1 red apple, cored
2 handfuls (50 g/1¾ oz) cavolo nero
   or curly kale, stems removed

a pinch of ground cayenne pepper
sea salt and freshly ground black
   pepper
2 free-range eggs

TO SERVE
sriracha sauce, gochujang, sweet chilli
   sauce or good-quality ketchup

Heat the oil in a medium-sized frying pan (skillet) on a medium heat. Finely slice the onion, add it to the pan and sauté for about 5 minutes or until it begins to soften.

Meanwhile, thinly slice the sweet potato, cut the Brussels sprouts in half and roughly chop the mushrooms. Add them to the pan and sauté for 5 more minutes.

Cut 5 of the tomatoes in half (leaving the others whole), thinly slice the apple and roughly chop the cavolo nero or kale. Add them to the pan along with the cayenne pepper, season to taste with salt and pepper and sauté for a further 5 minutes or until all of the vegetables are tender.

Create two small wells in the vegetable mixture and crack an egg into each one. Cook the eggs to your liking.

Serve straight from the pan, topped with a drizzle of spicy sauce or ketchup.

Raspberry Mousse
and Chia Parfait

Serves 2–4

Prep + cook time:
10 minutes

This is one of those happy coincidences when a really simple recipe also turns out to be deliciously addictive. The raspberry mousse is made with only three ingredients and it is easily something we could eat with a spoon straight from the food processor. However, turning it into a parfait by layering it with a spiced version of our chia pudding feels a little classier. Even though we placed this recipe in the breakfast chapter, it is often a midday snack and sometimes also a dessert in our home.

CHIA PUDDING
zest and juice of 1 small lime
½ batch (250 ml/8 fl oz/1 cup)
    Chia to Share (page 41)

RASPBERRY MOUSSE
200 g (7 oz/1½ cups) fresh raspberries,
    or frozen (thawed)
1 ripe avocado, stone removed and
    flesh scooped out
4 large soft dates, pitted

TO SERVE
cashew nut butter or Easy Nut Butter
    of choice (page 203)
fresh raspberries
desiccated unsweetened coconut

TIPS:
If you can't find soft dates, soak dried dates in hot water for 20 minutes.

For a nut-free alternative, replace the nut butter with a sunflower seed or pumpkin seed butter.

Add the lime zest and juice to the chia pudding and whisk until combined. Set aside while you prepare the raspberry mousse.

Place all of the raspberry mousse ingredients in a blender and blend on a high speed until completely smooth. To assemble, spoon the chia pudding into the base of two glasses and pour the mousse on top.

Serve topped with a dollop of nut butter, a few fresh raspberries and a sprinkling of coconut.

Golden Millet and Quinoa Porridge

Serves 4

Prep + cook time:
35 minutes

We have three different warm porridge recipes in this book (and one cold). It might sound like a lot but we could easily have added three more. Warm grains are one of our favourite ways to start the day, especially during the colder months. It feels so natural to us, as that is what we both had growing up in Scandinavia.

This porridge is made with two different seeds or pseudo-grains instead of grains. Millet and quinoa are cooked with a riot of warm spices to make a creamy and flavourful porridge that is rich in protein and great fuel that keeps us energised for hours. It's lush and warming, and the beautiful colour comes from turmeric. Always eat your porridge with a generous mix of toppings for a more interesting texture and flavour.

1 red apple, cored
100 g (3½ oz/½ cup) hulled uncooked millet, rinsed
90 g (3¼ oz/½ cup) white quinoa, rinsed
250 ml (8 fl oz/1 cup) plant-based milk of choice
½ tsp ground cinnamon
¼ tsp ground cardamom
¼ tsp ground ginger
½ tsp ground turmeric

a pinch of sea salt
1 tbsp honey

TO SERVE
sliced fresh apple
Easy Nut Butter of choice (page 203)
roughly chopped toasted nuts or seeds of choice
sultanas or raisins
raw cacao nibs
hemp seeds or bee pollen
plant-based milk of choice

Dice the apple and place it in a medium-sized saucepan along with the millet, quinoa, milk, 720 ml (24 fl oz/3 cups) of water, spices and salt. Bring to the boil, then reduce the heat and simmer for 15–20 minutes or until the millet is tender and little tails of the quinoa germ spiral out of the seed. Stir from time to time so the porridge doesn't burn on the base of the pan. Once cooked, remove from the heat and stir through the honey.

Serve topped with some apple slices, a dollop of nut butter, a sprinkling of nuts or seeds, sultanas or raisins, cacao nibs and hemp seeds or bee pollen, with a final splash of milk.

Herby Green Breakfast Bowl

Serves 2

Prep + cook time:
15 minutes

While a lot of our breakfasts lean towards the fruity/sweet or the rich oaty/grainy, this bowl is savoury and protein-packed yet also fresh and light. A base of quinoa and kale is studded with dill and parsley and topped with avocado, radishes and a soft-boiled egg. By simply rubbing the kale with oil and lemon, it softens without needing to be cooked, which not only saves time but also on dirty dishes. Before digging in, we sprinkle some Dukkah (page 202), Savoury Granola (page 200) or toasted seeds on top, for added flavour and crunch.

100 g (3½ oz/2 cups) curly kale, stems removed

1 tbsp extra-virgin olive oil, plus extra to drizzle

1 tbsp lemon juice

2 tbsp chopped fresh flat-leaf parsley leaves

2 tbsp chopped fresh dill

150 g (5¼ oz/1 cup) cooked Quick Quinoa (page 31) (or ½ cup uncooked, boiled in salted water for 15–18 minutes)

sea salt and freshly ground black pepper

TO SERVE

2 free-range eggs

2 ripe avocados, stones removed and flesh sliced

4 radishes, sliced

1 tbsp extra-virgin olive oil

2 tbsp Dukkah (page 202) or Savoury Granola (page 200)

Fill a small saucepan with water and bring to a boil. Add the eggs and let them cook for 6–7 minutes before removing from the heat. Rinse the eggs in cold water and carefully peel off the shells.

Meanwhile, roughly chop the kale and transfer it to a large mixing bowl. Add the oil and lemon juice and massage the kale for a minute or so or until the leaves begin to soften. Add the parsley and dill to the bowl along with the cooked quinoa. Season to taste with salt and pepper and stir until combined.

Divide between two bowls and serve topped with halved eggs, avocado and radish slices, a sprinkling of dukkah or granola, and a drizzle of oil.

TIP:
For a vegan alternative, simply leave out the egg.

Turmeric and Blueberry Muffins with Granola

Makes 12 muffins

Prep + cook time:
35 minutes

This is the ultimate breakfast muffin and one of the most popular recipes we have posted on the blog. Unlike most muffin recipes that are promoted as breakfast (even though they are in fact filled with sugar and are more like a dessert) these only have ingredients that you actually would eat for breakfast.

So, technically, this is oat porridge, banana pancakes and a bowl of buttermilk smashed together into beautifully golden muffins that are quick to make and taste out of this world. One or two grated carrots can also be a delicious addition.

DRY INGREDIENTS
100 g (3½ oz/1 cup) rolled oats
100 g (3½ oz/1 cup) walnuts
100 g (3½ oz/⅔ cup) buckwheat flour,
    plus 2 tbsp arrowroot
    (or potato starch) or 100 g (3½ oz/
    ⅔ cup) spelt flour
1 tbsp ground turmeric
1½ tsp baking powder
1 tsp ground cardamom
½ tsp bicarbonate of soda
    (baking soda)
½ tsp sea salt
a pinch of freshly ground black pepper

WET INGREDIENTS
2 ripe bananas, peeled
6 soft dates, pitted or 6 tbsp runny
    honey or pure maple syrup
160 ml (5½ fl oz/⅔ cup) buttermilk or
    full-fat plain unsweetened yoghurt
80 ml (2½ fl oz/⅓ cup) extra-virgin
    olive oil or butter, melted
3 free-range eggs
150 g (5¼ oz/1 cup) blueberries or
    berries of choice, fresh or frozen

FOR THE GRANOLA TOPPING
2 tbsp virgin coconut oil or butter
2 tbsp runny honey or pure maple
    syrup
60 g (2 oz/½ cup) rolled oats

TIPS:
If you can't find soft dates, soak dried dates in hot water for 20 minutes.

For a nut-free alternative, replace the walnuts with sunflower seeds.

For a vegan alternative, replace the buttermilk with a plant-based yoghurt and replace the eggs with 3 tbsp of chia seeds soaked in 9 tbsp of filtered water for 20 minutes.

Preheat the oven to 200°C (400°F/Gas mark 6) and grease a 12-hole muffin tin or line it with paper cup liners.

Place the oats and walnuts in a food processor and blend until the texture resembles coarse flour. Transfer to a large mixing bowl, add the rest of the dry ingredients and stir until combined. Make a well in the centre and set aside.

Mash the bananas and dates (or honey/maple syrup) with a fork and place them in the food processor along with the buttermilk or yoghurt, oil or butter, and eggs. Blend until smooth then pour into the well of the dry ingredients with the blueberries. Using a spatula, gently fold the wet ingredients into the dry ingredients until just combined, making sure not to over-mix.

To make the granola topping, melt the oil in a small saucepan on a low heat then remove from the heat. Add the honey and oats, stir until combined and set aside.

Fill the muffin tin with the batter and top each muffin with a tablespoon of the granola. Bake for about 20 minutes or until golden, turning the tin around halfway through cooking to ensure they bake evenly, and a skewer inserted in the centre of the muffins comes out clean. Remove from the oven and cool slightly in the tin before transferring to a wire rack to cool.

Store the muffins at room temperature in an airtight container and they will keep for a few days. Alternatively, freeze them.

Banana and Spinach Pancakes

Makes approx. 15 small
pancakes

Prep + cook time:
25 minutes

We always make this recipe in our high-speed blender – it's perfect for pancake batter, especially when they include bananas and spinach. Spinach pancakes have been one of our signature recipes for years but we've not shared one in our books before, so we're making up for it by including two different versions here.

These are thick, sweet and perfect for breakfast. The spinach not only adds colour but also gives them a hearty flavour that balances the sweetness of the bananas. The colour depends on the amount of spinach used and the heat of the pan (if the heat's too high it will make them brown).

4 free-range eggs
2 ripe bananas, peeled
120 ml (4 fl oz/½ cup) plant-based milk of choice
1 handful (25 g/¾ oz) baby spinach or frozen spinach, slightly thawed
15 fresh mint leaves (optional)
50 g (1¾ oz/½ cup) almond flour
60 g (2 oz/½ cup) buckwheat flour
40 g (1½ oz/½ cup) desiccated unsweetened coconut

1 tsp baking powder
a pinch of sea salt
virgin coconut oil or butter, to fry

TO SERVE
full-fat plain unsweetened yoghurt
pure maple syrup or honey (optional)
mixed berries of choice
fresh passion fruit pulp
seeds of choice, finely chopped

Crack the eggs into a blender, add the bananas, milk, spinach and mint (if using) and blend until well combined.

Add the dry ingredients, blend until completely smooth, then pour into a jug and leave the batter to rest for a few minutes.

Heat a little oil in a 20 cm (8 inch) non-stick frying pan (skillet) on a medium-high heat. Whisk the batter then ladle 60 ml (2 fl oz/¼ cup) for each pancake into the pan (you should be able to cook about 4 pancakes at a time). Fry for about 1½ minutes or until small bubbles appear on the surface and the bases are golden. Carefully flip each pancake with a spatula and fry the other side for a further minute or until golden. Transfer the cooked pancakes to a plate and repeat with the rest of the batter (you may need to reduce the heat slightly after the first batch).

Serve topped with a dollop of yoghurt, a drizzle of maple syrup, some berries and passion fruit pulp and a sprinkling of chopped seeds.

TIPS:
Alternatively, prepare the pancake batter in a large mixing bowl with a whisk or immersion (hand) blender. Just be sure to mash the bananas and finely chop the spinach and mint leaves (if using).

You can vary this recipe by replacing the spinach with berries of choice.

Baked Carrot Cake Oatmeal

Serves 8

Prep + cook time:
45 minutes

This is a family classic and instant favourite among many of our readers. We love baked porridge and included a berry version in our first book. This one flirts with the carrot cake concept, using shredded carrots, warm spices, sweetness from raisins – all of it tucked into an oaty cake topped with sweet and crunchy nuts and seeds.

We often make the recipe in a muffin tin and bake the muffins for a slightly shorter amount of time – they are also a hit. See tips below for a vegan version.

PORRIDGE
2 free-range eggs
500 ml (16 fl oz/2 cups) plant-based
    milk of choice (e.g. oat milk)
1 tsp baking powder
½ tsp ground cinnamon
½ tsp ground cardamom
½ tsp ground nutmeg
½ tsp ground ginger
½ tsp ground vanilla or
    2 tsp vanilla extract
a pinch of sea salt
200 g (7 oz) carrots, peeled
200 g (7 oz/2 cups) rolled oats
1 handful (50 g/1¾ oz) raisins

TOPPING
150 g (5¼ oz/1 cup) nuts of choice
    (e.g. walnuts, pecans or hazelnuts)
100 g (3½ oz/⅔ cup) pumpkin
    or sunflower seeds
3 tbsp pure maple syrup or runny
    honey
2 tbsp virgin coconut oil

TO SERVE
full-fat plain unsweetened yoghurt

Preheat the oven to 180°C (350°F/Gas mark 4) and grease a 30 × 20 × 5 cm (12 × 8 × 2 inch) ovenproof dish. Or a 25 cm (10 inch) round dish.

Crack the eggs into a large mixing bowl, add the milk, baking powder, spices, vanilla and salt and whisk until combined. Grate the carrots and transfer them to the bowl, add the oats and raisins and mix until combined. Pour the porridge into the dish and set aside while you prepare the topping.

Roughly chop the nuts, transfer to a medium-sized mixing bowl, add the rest of the topping ingredients and, using your hands, rub the oil and maple syrup or honey into the nuts and seeds until well coated. Scatter the topping over the porridge and bake for about 35 minutes or until the oats have absorbed the liquid and the topping is golden and crunchy.

Serve warm, topped with a dollop of yoghurt.

TIPS:
For a nut-free alternative, replace the nuts with more pumpkin or sunflower seeds.

For a vegan alternative, replace the eggs with 2 tbsp of chia seeds soaked in 6 tbsp of filtered water for 20 minutes.

Spectacular Rye Slices

Each recipe:
Serves 1

Prep + cook time:
5 minutes

Working out a recipe's popularity based on Instagram 'likes', reveals that various types of open-faced sandwiches with colourful toppings always spark a lot of attention! Often it seems like they are only made to be photographed, but we promise you that it is not the case here. These colourful slices are a collection of our favourite toppings. We like them on top of sourdough rye bread. For a gluten-free alternative, replace the sourdough rye bread with a gluten-free bread.

Avo and Za'atar

2 slices sourdough rye bread
1 ripe avocado, stone removed and
    flesh scooped out
2 tsp extra-virgin olive oil
1 tsp Za'atar (page 202)
    or ½ tsp chilli flakes
2 pinches of sea salt flakes

Toast the bread and finely slice the avocado. Drizzle the oil over the toast, fan out the avocado over the surface of the toast and gently press down with the back of a spoon. Sprinkle over the za'atar and salt and cut in half lengthwise.

Hazelnut Butter, Strawberry and Basil

2 slices sourdough rye bread
4 fresh strawberries, tops removed
2 tbsp hazelnut butter or Easy Nut
    Butter of choice (page 203)
2 pinches of freshly ground black
    pepper
8 fresh basil leaves

Toast the bread and finely slice the strawberries. Spread the nut butter over the toast and arrange the stberry slices over the surface of the toast. Sprinkle over the pepper, scatter over the basil and cut in half lengthwise.

Banana, Tahini and Honey

2 slices sourdough rye bread
1 ripe banana, peeled
2 tbsp butter (optional)
2 tsp tahini
2 tsp runny honey
1 tsp bee pollen

Toast the bread and finely slice the banana. Spread the butter over the toast (if using) and arrange the banana slices over the surface of the toast. Drizzle over the tahini and honey, sprinkle over the bee pollen and cut in half lengthwise.

Fig and Goat's Cheese

2 slices sourdough rye bread
2 fresh figs, tops removed
4 walnuts, toasted
2 tbsp soft goat's (chèvre) cheese
2 tsp runny honey
4 sprigs fresh thyme, leaves picked

TIPS:
For a nut-free alternative, replace the walnuts with pumpkin seeds or sunflower seeds.

For a vegan alternative, replace the goat's cheese with a vegan soft cheese and the honey with pure maple syrup.

Toast the bread, finely slice the figs and roughly chop the walnuts. Spread the goat's cheese over the toast and arrange the fig slices over the surface of the toast. Drizzle over the honey, scatter over the walnuts and thyme, and cut in half lengthwise.

Daily Green Smoothie

Serves 2

Prep + cook time:
5 minutes

We have written a whole book about smoothies, so we didn't want to include too many here (even if smoothies are one of our favourite breakfasts). Weirdly enough, this green smoothie didn't make it into the smoothie book even though it is always on repeat in our home. To be honest, David and the kids usually prefer pink, blue or purple berry smoothies in the morning, so I often get to have this one for myself.

It is packed with green vegetables but doesn't taste like grass at all. The lime and ginger make it fresh and the nut butter adds depth. When David does drink this, he usually throws a soft date in the blender as well, for extra sweetness. It is also great after a workout with the addition of a scoop of high-quality plant-based protein powder. *Luise*

1 ripe fresh or frozen banana, peeled
1 celery stalk (with leaves)
100 g (3½ oz/1 cup) fresh or frozen
   broccoli florets
1 handful (25 g/¾ oz) spinach, fresh
   or frozen

1 heaped tbsp Easy Nut Butter
   of choice (page 203)
1 tsp fresh ginger, peeled and grated
250 ml (8 fl oz/1 cup) plant-based milk
   of choice
juice of ½ lime

Roughly chop the banana and celery and transfer to a blender along with the rest of the ingredients. Blend on a high speed until completely smooth.

Pour into 2 medium-sized glasses and serve.

TIP:
For a nut-free alternative, replace the nut butter with a sunflower seed or pumpkin seed butter.

A Trio of Warm and Creamy Oats

Ring on our doorbell at around 7.15 a.m. on any random weekday and it's highly likely that you will find one of us in front of the stove, stirring a pan of oatmeal or porridge while the kids are banging their spoons on the table, chanting: '*Vi er sultne, vi er sultne!*' (We are hungry, we are hungry!). I am not sure what kind of marathon they run in their sleep, but they always wake up starving. Oatmeal is great in that sense, as it only takes a few minutes to cook and is packed with energy. Finish with a drizzle of honey if you prefer it sweeter.

Carrot and Rye Oatmeal

Serves 2

Prep + cook time:
15 minutes

APPLE COMPOTE
1 apple, cored
2 tbsp lemon juice
1 tsp runny honey (optional)
¼ tsp ground vanilla or
   1 tsp vanilla extract
¼ tsp ground cinnamon
¼ tsp fresh ginger, peeled and grated,
   or ⅛ tsp ground ginger

CARROT AND RYE OATMEAL
60 g (2 oz/½ cup) rolled oats
60 g (2 oz/½ cup) rye flakes
360 ml (12 fl oz/1½ cups)
   fresh carrot juice
250 ml (8 fl oz/1 cup) unsweetened
   plant-based milk of choice or water
a pinch of sea salt

TO SERVE
sultanas or raisins
raw cacao nibs
toasted flaxseeds, colour of choice

To prepare the apple compote, cut the apple into cubes, transfer to a small saucepan, add the rest of the apple compote ingredients, plus 2 tablespoons of water, cover, bring to the boil, reduce the heat and simmer for about 5 minutes, stirring from time to time, until tender and golden and the liquid has reduced.

Meanwhile, place all of the oatmeal ingredients in a medium-sized saucepan, bring to the boil, reduce the heat and simmer for about 5 minutes or until thick and creamy, stirring from time to time so the oatmeal doesn't burn on the base of the pan.

Serve the oatmeal topped with a spoonful of the apple compote and a sprinkling of sultanas or raisins, cacao nibs and flaxseeds.

Protein-boosted Oatmeal

Serves 2

Prep + cook time:
10 minutes

1 free-range egg
100 g (3½ oz/1 cup) rolled oats
360 ml (12 fl oz/1½ cups) plant-based
    milk of choice
½ tsp ground vanilla or
    2 tsp vanilla extract
a pinch of sea salt

TO SERVE
full-fat plain unsweetened yoghurt
    of choice
sliced ripe avocado
fresh raspberries
hemp seeds
chia seeds, colour of choice

Crack the egg into a medium-sized saucepan and whisk until combined. Add the rest of the oatmeal ingredients plus 250 ml (8 fl oz/1 cup) of water, bring to the boil, reduce the heat and simmer for about 5 minutes or until thick and creamy, stirring from time to time so the oatmeal doesn't burn on the base of the pan. Serve topped with a dollop of yoghurt, some avocado slices and raspberries and a sprinkling of hemp seeds and chia seeds.

Sweet Coconut Oatmeal

Serves 2

Prep + cook time:
10 minutes

120 g (4¼ oz/1 cup) rolled oats
360 ml (12 fl oz/1½ cups) coconut milk
a pinch of sea salt

TO SERVE
cacao and hazelnut butter or Easy
    Nut Butter of choice (page 203)
sliced fresh strawberries
roughly chopped toasted hazelnuts
toasted sunflower and pumpkin seeds
toasted desiccated unsweetened
    coconut
goji berries

TIP:
For a nut-free alternative, replace the nut butter with a sunflower seed or pumpkin seed butter and replace the hazelnuts with more sunflower seeds and pumpkin seeds.

Place all of the oatmeal ingredients in a medium-sized saucepan plus 250 ml (8 fl oz/1 cup) of water, bring to the boil, reduce the heat and simmer for about 5 minutes or until thick and creamy, stirring from time to time so the oatmeal doesn't burn on the base of the pan.

Serve topped with a dollop of nut butter, some strawberries and a sprinkling of hazelnuts, seeds, coconut and goji berries.

Flatbread Sandwiches with Hummus and Carrot Slaw

Serves 4

Prep + cook time:
15 minutes

This super-quick carrot slaw has distinct tones of mint and coriander and is really tasty sandwiched between two flatbreads slathered with hummus. The slaw can be prepared ahead and stored in the fridge, but we often just make a casual version in the morning with a hand grater and a chopping board. If you have some sumac or Za'atar (page 202) in the store cupboard, go ahead and add a sprinkle of that as well.

FOR THE CARROT SLAW
¼ red onion, peeled
2 tbsp lemon juice
1 tbsp olive oil
2 carrots, trimmed, tops removed
    and peeled
1 handful (25 g/¾ oz) fresh coriander
    (cilantro) and mint, leaves picked
2 tbsp raisins
sea salt and freshly ground black
    pepper

TO SERVE
8 slices Rainbow Flatbreads (page 38)
    (green broccoli version pictured),
    or bread of choice
Heavenly Hummus (page 26)
thinly sliced cucumber, or radish
lettuce leaves

To prepare the slaw, thinly slice the onion, transfer to a medium-sized mixing bowl, massage with the lemon juice and oil and set aside.

Meanwhile, grate the carrots and roughly chop the herbs then transfer to the bowl of onion, along with the raisins. Season to taste with salt and pepper and mix until combined.

To assemble, spread 8 flatbread slices with some hummus, arrange slaw, cucumber or radish and lettuce on top of 4 of them and cover with the remaining 4 flatbreads. Wrap some parchment paper around the sandwiches to keep the filling in place.

Buckwheat and Blueberry Bircher

Serves 2

Prep + cook time:
10 minutes + soaking
overnight

One of the worst comments we have received about a recipe was in an email from a reader telling us that even though she appreciated the flavour of our overnight buckwheat porridge, the texture felt like eating grainy sand! FAIL!

Her version was probably not blended thoroughly enough, but to avoid any more sand incidents we came up with a recipe where the soaked buckwheat, almonds and sunflower seeds are not blended at all – instead, they are simply stirred together with yoghurt, fruit and spices. The result is a unique Bircher with a chewy texture and fresh flavour.

50 g (1¾ oz/¼ cup) buckwheat
40 g (1½ oz/¼ cup) almonds
40 g (1½ oz/¼ cup) sunflower seeds
1 red apple, cored
250 ml (8 fl oz/1 cup) full-fat plain
   unsweetened yoghurt
1 tbsp pure maple syrup or runny
   honey (optional)
1 tbsp lemon juice

1 tsp fresh ginger, peeled and grated,
   or ½ tsp ground ginger
½ tsp ground cinnamon
75 g (2¾ oz/½ cup) blueberries,
   fresh or frozen (thawed)

TO SERVE
fresh or frozen blueberries (thawed)
fresh raspberries
Easy Nut Butter of choice (page 203)
bee pollen

Place the buckwheat, almonds and seeds in a sealable glass jar, cover with 360 ml (12 fl oz/1½ cups) of water and set aside in the fridge to soak for at least 1 hour, or overnight.

Drain and rinse the activated buckwheat, almonds and seeds and transfer to a medium-sized mixing bowl. Finely dice the apple and add it to the bowl along with the yoghurt, maple syrup or honey (if using), lemon juice, ginger and cinnamon and mix until combined. Stir through the blueberries to create a marbled effect.

Serve topped with more blueberries, some raspberries, a dollop of nut butter and a sprinkling of bee pollen.

TIPS:
For a nut-free alternative, replace the almonds with pumpkin seeds.

For a vegan alternative, replace the yoghurt with a plant-based yoghurt such as coconut, soy or oat.

Banana and Cacao Granola

Makes approx. 700 g
(1½ lb/5 cups)

Prep + cook time:
30 minutes

You know you've got a good granola recipe on hand when you travel to the other side of the globe and meet someone randomly who starts talking about it. That happened to us in St Kilda, Melbourne: the guy working at an ice-cream parlour recognised us because our Banana Granola was his favourite recipe and he had made a batch that morning. Then and there, we decided that we had to include the recipe in our next book. To make the original recipe even better, we have given it a chocolate twist.

What makes our granola special is that the oats and nuts are mixed with mashed bananas and cacao, giving it the perfect balance of crunchy and chewy. It is slightly sweet and divinely delicious. It is very easy to make, too.

DRY INGREDIENTS
75 g (2¾ oz/½ cup) almonds
60 g (2 oz/½ cup) pecans
300 g (10½ oz/3 cups) rolled oats
75 g (2¾ oz/½ cup) pumpkin seeds
3 tbsp raw cacao powder
¼ tsp ground vanilla or
   1 tsp vanilla extract
2 pinches of sea salt

WET INGREDIENTS
5 tbsp virgin coconut oil
5 tbsp pure maple syrup, runny honey
   or date molasses
2 very ripe bananas, peeled

TO SERVE
milk of choice or plain unsweetened
   yoghurt of choice
chopped fresh fruit of choice

Preheat the oven to 200°C (400°F/Gas mark 6) and line a baking tray with parchment paper. Roughly chop the nuts, and add them to a large mixing bowl along with the rest of the dry ingredients. Stir until combined and set aside.

Melt the oil and maple syrup, honey or molasses in a small saucepan on a low heat. Mash the bananas, add them to the pan and stir until combined. Pour the wet ingredients over the dry ingredients and, using your hands or a spatula, mix until well combined and clumpy.

Spread the granola out in a single layer on the baking tray and bake for 15–20 minutes or until golden. Stir it from time to time to prevent it from burning. Remove from the oven and set aside to cool completely.

Serve with a dash of milk and/or a dollop of yoghurt and some fresh fruit.

Store the granola at room temperature in a large sealable glass jar and it will keep for a month or so.

TIP:
For a nut-free alternative, replace the almonds with sunflower seeds, white sesame seeds or black chia seeds.

Fruit-flavoured Yoghurt Pots

Each recipe:
Serves 2

Prep + cook time:
10 minutes

'Daddy, can we buy that? Pleeeeeease!' Elsa is pointing at eight colourful yoghurt packages with fun animations on them. Passing the yoghurt and cereal sections in the supermarket with the kids always means trouble. Those cartoon figures on the boxes do a stellar job of convincing children that their parents should buy them. If I were a kid I would also want them. But now I am the adult and I know that even if they are supposed to contain fruit yoghurt, the yoghurt pots are mostly filled with sugar, preservatives and artificial fruit flavours. Delicious as they might be, we'd rather give our kids a breakfast that sustains them for longer and contains vitamins, and ingredients that won't turn them into bouncing balls within 15 minutes.

Our homemade fruit-flavoured yoghurt pots might not feature cartoon figures but they do taste a lot like the real (or should I say fake) thing. We mix plain yoghurt with real fruit to get a mix of colours and flavours and store them in small glass jars in the fridge. The trick to making thick, creamy flavoured yoghurts is to mix the flavours in the blender (if they require blending), not the yoghurt. If the yoghurt is mixed in the blender it immediately becomes too liquid.

Depending on the type of yoghurt you use, you'll get a thicker or runnier consistency. Greek or Turkish yoghurt will give you the creamiest result, but any type of yoghurt will work. If you are making the Strawberry and Vanilla Yoghurt (opposite) and strawberries are in season, choose fresh ripe ones and organic if possible (strawberries are heavily sprayed). If they are not in season, buy frozen strawberries and thaw them before blending. Frozen fruit and vegetables are picked when ripe and frozen very shortly after being picked, which means they containing a high amount of nutrients compared to the store-bought fresh ones. *Luise*

Orange Yoghurt with Honey and Ginger Seeds

ORANGE YOGHURT
500 ml (16 fl oz/2 cups) thick, full-fat
    plain unsweetened yoghurt
juice of 1 orange (about 120 ml/4 fl oz/
    ½ cup)
1 tsp ground cardamom

HONEY AND GINGER SEEDS
2 tbsp runny honey
2 tbsp seeds of choice (e.g. sesame
    seeds, poppy seeds, hemp seeds,
    linseeds, sunflower seeds,
    pumpkin seeds)
½ tsp ground ginger

Place all of the orange yoghurt ingredients in a medium-sized mixing bowl, mix until combined and set aside. Place all of the honey and ginger seeds ingredients in a small bowl and mix until combined.

Pour half of the honey yoghurt into a medium-sized sealable glass jar (or more smaller jars) and top with the orange and ginger seeds. Use the back of a spoon to create a ripple effect between the two layers, then cover with the rest of the yoghurt. Alternatively, add the honey and ginger seeds to the bottom or top of the jar. Store the yoghurt in the fridge in a sealed container and it will keep for a few days.

Strawberry and Vanilla Yoghurt

225 g (7¾ oz/1½ cups) strawberries,
    fresh or frozen (thawed)
2 soft dates, pitted, or 2 tsp date
    molasses

¼ tsp ground vanilla or
    1 tsp vanilla extract
500 ml (16 fl oz/2 cups) thick, full-fat
    plain unsweetened yoghurt

Place the strawberries, dates and vanilla in a food processor or blender and mix until smooth. Reserve a few tablespoons of strawberry sauce and transfer the rest to a medium-sized mixing bowl, add the yoghurt and mix until combined.

Pour the strawberry and vanilla yoghurt into a medium-sized sealable glass jar (or more smaller jars) and stir in the reserved strawberry sauce for a ripple effect. Store in the fridge, sealed, and it will keep for a few days.

Blueberry and Cherry Yoghurt

75 g (2¾ oz/½ cup) blueberries, fresh or frozen (thawed)
75 g (2¾ oz/½ cup) cherries, fresh or frozen (thawed)
½ ripe banana, peeled

500 ml (16 fl oz/2 cups) thick, full-fat plain unsweetened yoghurt
25 g (¾ oz/¼ cup) desiccated unsweetened coconut

Place the blueberries, cherries and banana in a food processor or blender and mix until smooth. Transfer to a medium-sized mixing bowl, add the yoghurt and coconut and mix until combined.

Pour the blueberry and cherry yoghurt into a medium-sized sealable glass jar (or more smaller jars). Store in the fridge, sealed, and it will keep for a few days.

Mango and Banana Yoghurt with Passion Fruit

½ mango, stone removed and flesh scooped out
½ ripe banana, peeled
juice of ½ lime

500 ml (16 fl oz/2 cups) thick, full-fat plain unsweetened yoghurt
1 passion fruit, flesh scooped out

Place the mango flesh, banana and lime juice in a food processor or blender and mix until smooth. Transfer to a medium-sized mixing bowl, add the yoghurt and stir until combined.

Pour half of the mango and banana yoghurt into a medium-sized sealable glass jar (or more smaller jars) and top with the passion fruit. Use the back of a spoon to create a ripple effect between the two layers, then cover with the rest of the yoghurt. Alternatively, add the passion fruit to the bottom or top of the jar. Store the yoghurt in the fridge, sealed, and it will keep for a few days.

Gluten-free Veggie Buns

Makes 12 buns

Prep + cook time:
30 minutes + 1 hour
baking

This recipe is a good introduction to gluten-free bread baking. These little buns are very easy to prepare and contain no egg, butter, nuts or yeast (and therefore they don't need any kneading or leavening time). They are flavoured with vegetables and when baked right, they have a nice crust and a softly textured crumb without being crumbly like many other gluten-free breads are. This is thanks to the psyllium the magic fibre that holds the bread together. It is also really good for your gut.

3 tbsp psyllium husks or 2 tbsp
   psyllium husk powder
500 ml (16 fl oz/2 cups) filtered water
   or plant-based milk of choice
2 tbsp extra-virgin olive oil
1 tsp sea salt
110 g (3¾ oz/1½ cups) rolled oats
120 g (4¼ oz/1 cup) buckwheat flour
140 g (5 oz/1 cup) rice flour, plus extra
   to dust
1½ tsp baking powder

VEGETABLE OPTIONS
[Option 1] 1 carrot plus 1 parsnip,
   grated (150 g/5¼ oz)
[Option 2] 70 g (2½ oz/1 packed cup)
   fresh spinach, chopped plus 1 ripe
   banana, peeled and mashed
[Option 3] 1–2 beetroots (beets),
   peeled and grated (130 g/4½ oz) plus
   4 soft dates, pitted and mashed

SEED TOPPING
extra-virgin olive oil (to brush)
35 g (1¼ oz/¼ cup) seeds of choice

The baking time can vary quite a bit, depending on your oven, the size of the buns and how many sheets you are baking at the same time.

TIP:
Psyllium can be found in the gluten-free section of larger supermarkets, health food stores or online.

If you can't find soft dates, soak dried dates in hot water for 20 minutes.

Preheat the oven to 190°C (375°F/Gas mark 5) and line a baking tray with parchment paper.

Place the psyllium husks and water or milk in a mixing bowl, stir to combine then set aside until the mixture becomes viscous and gel-like. Whisk vigorously to incorporate as much air as possible.

Add your vegetable option to the bowl along with the oil and salt and combine. Fold in the oats, flours and baking powder and form into a sticky dough before rolling it into a log. Divide the dough into 12 pieces and, using damp hands, shape them into buns. Place them on the baking tray, brush with oil, sprinkle with seeds and bake for 40–60 minutes,* until they form a golden crust and are firm to touch.

Remove from the oven and set aside to cool a little before slicing open. Serve slightly warm filled with lashings of butter, nut butter or mashed avocado. Store the buns at room temperature in a bread bin or wrapped. They will keep for a few days. Alternatively, pre-slice the buns and freeze them.

Handy Meals

When our daughter was still in preschool they had forest hikes on Fridays. Somehow, it had become an unwritten rule that all kids got crêpe rolls in their lunchboxes every week! We still can't understand how the kids could convince their parents to do this (or if it was just Elsa that had us fooled), but since we didn't want her to be the only kid without crêpes, we gave in to the pressure. To make sure that she also ate some vegetables, we made different colours of crêpes every week – green spinach (page 127), yellow carrot (page 97) and pink beetroot (page 219), or added fillings to the crêpe rolls. We also threw in some carrot sticks on the side and a small box of chickpeas (garbanzo beans) or sunflower seeds.

In this chapter you'll find more than crêpe rolls, though. We are sharing meals that travel well in a lunchbox and are nice to bring to a picnic or potluck. Whether you decide on our vegetable-packed pasta salad with creamy pesto and avocado dressing (page 92), the Middle Eastern wraps with sweet potato coins (page 95) or our favourite Spinach and Feta Quiche (page 105), these are all dishes that stay fresh for a couple of hours and can be enjoyed both warm or cold. *Luise*

Mushroom and Cauliflower 'Rice' Sushi Rolls

Serves 4 (about 40 pieces/4 rolls)

Prep + cook time: 35 minutes

Ever since we started turning cauliflower into 'rice', sushi-making has become a whole lot easier. The added tahini, rice vinegar, maple syrup and sesame oil make the 'rice' surprisingly sticky and give it the characteristic sushi flavours.

CAULIFLOWER SUSHI 'RICE'
1 cauliflower head (approx. 900 g/2 lb)
3 tbsp rice vinegar
2 tbsp tahini
1 tbsp pure maple syrup
1 tbsp sesame seed oil
¼ tsp sea salt

SAUTÉED MUSHROOMS
200 g (7 oz) brown mushrooms, cleaned
1 tbsp sesame seed oil
½ tsp sea salt
¼ tsp freshly ground black pepper

FILLING
4 nori sheets
1 firm but ripe avocado, stone removed, flesh scooped out
10 cm (4 inch) piece cucumber, sliced into thin strips (organic if possible)
½ red (bell) pepper, core and seeds removed and sliced into thin strips
2 tbsp black sesame seeds

TO SERVE
black sesame seeds
pickled ginger
wasabi
GMO-free organic soy or tamari sauce

Boil some water in a kettle or electric jug. Pulse the cauliflower florets in a food processor until the texture resembles rice. Transfer to a sieve set over the sink, pour over the boiled water and drain thoroughly. Put in a bowl with the rest of the cauliflower 'rice' ingredients and mix well. Set aside in the fridge.

Thinly slice the mushrooms. Heat the oil in a frying pan (skillet) on a medium-high heat, add the mushrooms, salt and pepper, and sauté until golden and tender. Stir them every now and again then remove from the heat and set aside to cool.

Place a nori sheet, shiny side down, on a bamboo sushi mat. Spread a quarter of the 'rice' evenly over two-thirds of the sheet (about 5 mm/⅛ inch thick).

Cut the avocado into thin strips. Begin by filling the centre of the 'rice' with a line of the avocado, then top with some cucumber, pepper, mushrooms and finally a sprinkling of sesame seeds. Lifting the front of the sushi mat, gently but tightly roll the sheet, sealing the end with a little water. Set aside in the fridge while you assemble the other three sheets. Use a sharp knife dipped in hot water to slice the sushi into 2 cm (¾ inch) rolls. Sprinkle with black sesame seeds and serve with ginger, wasabi and soy sauce.

TIPS:
Cremini, oyster or shiitake mushrooms work well.

If you don't have a bamboo sushi mat, simply use a piece of cling film (plastic wrap) on top of a folded tea towel.

Mediterranean Salad Jar

Serves 2

Prep + cook time:
10 minutes

Isn't the whole idea of salad jars just excellent? Place the dressing in the bottom of the jar and fill it up with your favourite mix of vegetables, grains, legumes and fruit. Easy to prepare, perfect to transport, they last a couple of days in the fridge and you get to do the bartender-shake to get the dressing covering all the veggies. Our Mediterranean salad jar uses simple pesto as a dressing and is filled with yummy marinated veggies and beans, beautiful, crunchy Chioggia beetroot (beet), spiralized courgette (zucchini) and sweet fresh figs.

1 raw Chioggia beetroot (beet), peeled
8 black Kalamata olives, drained and pitted
1 courgette (zucchini)
2 small figs or 8 seedless grapes
8 cherry tomatoes
4 tbsp Perfect Pesto (page 25) or store-bought pesto

2 tbsp olive oil
8 pieces marinated artichoke hearts, drained
70 g (2½ oz/½ cup) tinned beans (white, borlotti or kidney), rinsed and drained
2 handfuls (50 g/1¾ oz) mixed salad leaves
2 tbsp lemon juice

Wash and dry all of the fresh produce. Thinly slice the beetroot (use a mandoline if you have one), cut the olives in half, spiralize or shred the courgette, cut the figs into quarters (or the grapes in half) and halve the tomatoes.

Whisk together pesto and olive oil to loosen it. Spoon the pesto into the base of two medium-sized wide-mouth sealable glass jars. Arrange the beetroot slices around the inside of the jars. Fill the jars with the olives and marinated artichokes, then the beans, followed by the courgette, fruit and tomatoes and finally the salad leaves and lemon juice squeezed on top.

Seal the jars to take on a picnic or store them in the fridge. They can keep for a few days in the fridge, if unopened.

When ready to serve, shake the salad out into a bowl and toss gently until coated in the pesto. Alternatively, shake and eat straight from the jar with a fork!

Broccoli, Spinach and Apple Muffins

Makes 12 muffins

Prep + cook time:
1 hour

We created these muffins as a quick snack for our children. Broccoli is Elsa's all-time favourite vegetable and muffins are one of her preferred treats. Here we add apple for a touch of sweetness, as well as honey and Dijon mustard for a delicious flavour twist.

VEGETABLE FILLING
½ leek (approx. 85 g/3 oz)
½ broccoli (approx. 150 g/5¼ oz)
2 tbsp extra-virgin olive oil
2 garlic cloves, peeled and finely chopped
1 tsp finely chopped fresh thyme or oregano
½ tsp sea salt
¼ tsp freshly ground black pepper
1 cooking apple, cored and cut into 1 cm (½ inch) cubes
1 large handful (30 g/1 oz) spinach, roughly chopped

DRY INGREDIENTS
160 g (5¾ oz/1 cup) buckwheat flour
100 g (3¼ oz/1 cup) rolled oats
2 tbsp arrowroot (or potato starch)
2 tsp baking powder
½ tsp sea salt

WET INGREDIENTS
3 free-range eggs
160 ml (5½ fl oz/⅔ cup) plain unsweetened yoghurt
120 ml (4 fl oz/½ cup) extra-virgin olive oil
1 tbsp good-quality honey
1 tbsp wholegrain Dijon mustard
2 tsp organic unfiltered apple cider vinegar

TOPPING
pumpkin seeds

TIPS:
Try adding some crumbled feta on top along with the pumpkin seeds.

For a vegan alternative, replace the dairy yoghurt with a plant-based yoghurt, and replace the eggs with 3 tbsp of chia seeds soaked for at least 30 minutes in 9 tbsp of filtered water.

Preheat the oven to 200°C (400°F/Gas mark 6), grease a large 12-hole muffin tin or two smaller 6-hole ones and line with parchment paper or paper cup liners. Alternatively, use a silicone muffin tin.

Wash and finely chop the leek, trim and finely chop the broccoli stalk and roughly chop the florets. Heat the oil for the filling in a frying pan (skillet) on a medium heat. Add the leek and broccoli stalk and sauté for 5 minutes. Add the broccoli florets, along with the garlic, thyme and salt and pepper and sauté for

continues overleaf

a further 5 minutes. Lastly, add the apple along with the spinach and sauté until the other vegetables have softened, the apple is tender and the spinach has wilted. Stir occasionally, to prevent the vegetables and apple from burning. Remove from the heat and set aside while you prepare the dry ingredients.

Put all of the dry ingredients in a food processor and blend on a high speed until well combined and the oats resemble coarse flour. Transfer to a large bowl, make a well in the centre and set aside while you prepare the wet ingredients.

Crack the eggs, add them to the food processor along with the rest of the wet ingredients and blend on a high speed until well combined. Pour the wet ingredients into the well of the dry ingredients and, using a spatula, start folding the wet ingredients into the dry ingredients. Add the broccoli, spinach and apple filling and gently fold until just combined, making sure not to over-mix as this will make the muffins tough.

Divide the batter evenly between the cups of the muffin tin, sprinkle with some pumpkin seeds and bake for about 20 minutes or until golden and a skewer inserted in the centre of one of the muffins comes out clean. Turn the tin around halfway through the cooking time to ensure that the muffins bake evenly.

Remove the muffins from the oven and set aside to cool slightly in the tin before transferring to a wire rack to cool completely or devouring them while still warm.

They can keep for a few days if stored in an airtight container at room temperature. They also freeze well.

Strawberry and Pesto Pasta Salad

Serves 6

Prep + cook time:
30 minutes

Pasta salad has got a pretty bad rep thanks to the heavy mayo and ham salads from the 90s. Our modern version is easy on the eye and much fresher, with a bounty of fruit and veggies to complement the pasta. Mixing pesto with avocado for the dressing makes it creamy, rich and flavourful yet still light.

300 g (10½ oz/3 cups) wholegrain or gluten-free pasta of choice
1 broccoli, head and stalk
2 carrots, tops removed and peeled
250 g (8¾ oz/1½ cups) fresh strawberries, tops removed
250 g (8¾ oz/2 cups) cherry tomatoes
1 × 400 g (14 oz) tin chickpeas (garbanzo beans),* drained and rinsed
1 handful (25 g/¾ oz) fresh basil, leaves picked

PESTO AND AVOCADO DRESSING
75 g (2¾ oz/⅓ cup) Perfect Pesto (page 25) or store-bought pesto
1 ripe avocado, stone removed and flesh scooped out
4 tbsp extra-virgin olive oil
juice of ½ lemon
sea salt and freshly ground black pepper

TO SERVE
shaved slices of pecorino, Grana Padano or Parmigiano Reggiano
toasted pine nuts
sea salt and freshly ground black pepper
extra-virgin olive oil

* Or 200 g (7 oz/1½ cups) cooked chickpeas (garbanzo beans) (page 26).

TIPS:
For a nut-free alternative, replace the pine nuts with pumpkin seeds or sunflower seeds.

For a vegan alternative, replace the pecorino with a vegan hard cheese.

Bring a large pan of water to the boil. Add a generous pinch of salt and the pasta, stir, and cook until al dente.

Meanwhile, cut the broccoli into small florets, trim and roughly chop the stalk and place them in a sieve over the pasta water during the last few minutes of cooking. Drain the pasta and broccoli and set aside to cool slightly.

Place all of the dressing ingredients in a medium-sized bowl, season to taste, mash until combined and set aside.

Thinly slice the carrots, cut the strawberries into quarters and the tomatoes in half. Transfer the pasta and broccoli to a large serving bowl, add the rest of the ingredients along with the dressing and gently toss until everything is well coated. Add a dash of water if you need to loosen the dressing. Serve topped with some pecorino, a sprinkling of pine nuts, seasoning and a drizzle of oil.

Middle Eastern
Sweet Potato Wraps

Serves 2

Prep + cook time:
35 minutes

We didn't grow up eating sweet potatoes, as they have only become popular in Scandinavia during the last decade. But we sure are making up for it now.

Roasted sweet potato slices are on weekly rotation in our home and we use them in a variety of recipes – tucking them into salads, mixing them with cooked lentils as a hearty dinner, placing them inside mayo sandwiches, or in wraps like this one here. The boiled eggs make it a more substantial meal; dates, pomegranate, feta add a burst of flavours and lettuce and cucumber keep it light and fresh. A green smoothie (page 63) is the perfect accompaniment.

1 small sweet potato
½ tsp ground cumin
¼ tsp ground turmeric
½ tsp sea salt
¼ tsp freshly ground black pepper
2 tbsp extra-virgin olive oil
2 wholegrain or buckwheat tortillas
   or flatbreads
2 small handfuls (50 g/1¾ oz)
   mixed lettuce

10 cucumber slices
2 free-range hard-boiled eggs, peeled
   and quartered
2 soft dates, pitted and thinly sliced
40 g (1½ oz) feta, crumbled
¼ pomegranate, seeded
2 tbsp tahini
sea salt and freshly ground black
   pepper

Preheat the oven to 200°C (400°F/Gas mark 6) and line a baking tray with parchment paper.

Wash and dry the sweet potato then slice it into 5 mm (⅛ inch) thick rounds (with the skin on). Put the rounds in a bowl along with the spices, salt, pepper and oil and toss until well coated. Spread the sweet potato out in a single layer on the baking tray and bake for 20–30 minutes or until soft and golden with crispy edges. Turn the slices over halfway through the cooking time to ensure that they bake evenly. Remove from the oven and set aside while you start assembling the tortillas.

Heat the tortillas in the oven for a couple of minutes then lay them flat on a board. Fill the centre of each tortilla with a line of the lettuce, then top with the baked sweet potato, followed by the cucumber, eggs, dates and feta and, finally, a sprinkling of the pomegranate seeds, a drizzle of the tahini and a pinch of the salt and pepper. Gently fold the bottom of each tortilla up to cover part of the filling, before folding one side in towards the centre, followed by the other. Enjoy!

TIP:
If you can't find soft dates, soak dried dates in hot water for 20 minutes.

Korean Carrot Crêpe Rolls

Makes 10–12 crêpes

Prep + cook time:
50 minutes

This is a twist on our Rice Crêpe Batter (page 32) and it demonstrates how very varied it can be. We add carrots to the batter before frying the crêpes, then we stuff them with a Korean-inspired filling and serve them like spring rolls. It takes a little effort to chop all the vegetables and roll the crêpes but it's totally worth it. This one is great enjoyed with friends – one fries the pancakes while another chops the vegetables, then you all sit and roll and eat together by the table. They also pack well in a lunchbox.

CARROT CRÊPES
1 quantity Rice Crêpe Batter
   (page 32)
80 g (3 oz) carrots, peeled
virgin coconut oil or butter, to fry

FOR THE RAW VEGGIE FILLING
2 carrots, tops removed and peeled
100 g (3½ oz) mangetout (snow peas),
   trimmed
¼ small red cabbage, trimmed
1 ripe avocado, stone removed and
   flesh scooped out

FOR THE MARINATED TOFU
½–1 fresh red chilli, seeded
3 tbsp tamari or soy sauce
2 tbsp rice vinegar
1 tbsp sesame seed oil
1 tbsp fresh ginger, peeled and grated
200 g (7 oz) organic firm tofu, drained
virgin coconut oil or butter, to fry

TO SERVE
kimchi
fresh coriander (cilantro) leaves
toasted sesame seeds
lime wedges
runny honey
peanut butter, or Easy Nut Butter
   of choice (page 203)

Put the crêpe batter in a blender or food processor. Grate the carrots, transfer to the blender, blend until completely smooth and slightly orange.

Meanwhile, prepare the raw veggie filling. Julienne the carrots and mangetout, thinly slice the cabbage and avocado and transfer to a serving plate.

To prepare the marinated tofu, roughly chop the chilli, transfer to a small serving bowl along with the tamari or soy sauce, vinegar, sesame seed oil and ginger, whisk until combined and set aside. Cut the tofu lengthwise into 1 cm (½ inch) thick slices. Heat a little oil or butter in a 20 cm (8 inch) non-stick

TIP:
Alternatively, prepare the crêpe batter in a large mixing bowl with a whisk or immersion (hand) blender blender; just be sure to finely grate the carrot first.

continues overleaf

frying pan (skillet) on a medium-high heat. Once hot, add the tofu and fry for about 5 minutes or until golden on the underside. Turn the tofu over and fry for a further 5 minutes or so, until golden. Transfer to a serving dish, drizzle over some of the marinade, reserving the rest to serve, toss to coat and set aside while you cook the crêpes.

Heat a little oil or butter in the same 20 cm (8 inch) non-stick frying pan on a medium-high heat. Once hot, whisk the batter then ladle 80 ml (2½ fl oz/⅓ cup) into the pan, tilting the pan to spread and evenly distribute the batter. Fry for 1–2 minutes or until small bubbles form on the surface and the base is golden. Carefully flip the crêpe with a spatula and fry the other side for a further 1–2 minutes or until cooked and golden. Transfer the cooked crêpe to a plate and repeat with the rest of the batter (you may need to reduce the heat slightly after the first crêpe).

Serve the crêpes topped with some veggies, tofu, kimchi, a scattering of coriander, sprinkling of sesame seeds, squeeze of lime juice and a drizzle of honey. Roll up, seal with a dollop of peanut butter and cut in half. Eat them with your hands, using the remaining tofu marinade as dipping sauce.

Beetroot and Chia Juice

Serves 2

Prep + cook time:
10 minutes + 1 hour
chilling time

Earthy beetroot (beet) mixed with sweet apples, tangy lemon, cucumber and celery is the base of this very tasty juice. But the flavour is probably not what's on your mind after your first sip. You will instead be preoccupied by that unusual feeling on your tongue from the jelly-like chia seeds that are floating in the juice. They are a rather unexpected sensation in a drink (unless you live in Asia, where they often mix jellified seeds into liquids). Once you get used to the feeling you'll quickly realise that it's quite addictive and pleasant. The chia seeds also add a rare quality to a juice – not only does it satisfy thirst but it also stills hunger, as the seeds are high in protein.

4 raw beetroots (beets), tops
    removed and peeled
2 red apples, cored
½ cucumber (organic if possible)
2 celery stalks with tops
1 lemon, peeled
4 tbsp chia seeds, colour
    of choice

Wash the fruit and vegetables and roughly chop them so they fit your juicer. Feed them through the mouth of the juicer one by one, using the hard ingredients (e.g. beetroot, apple, cucumber, celery) to push the juicy ingredients (e.g. lemon) through. Taste and adjust the flavours to your liking.

Add the chia seeds and stir well. Pour into two medium-sized sealable glass bottles (as featured in the photo) and store in the fridge for about 1 hour, or until the juice is chilled and the chia seeds have absorbed some of the liquid.

Roasted Root Frittata Muffins

Makes 12 muffins

Prep + cook time:
30 minutes

We all need a few kitchen hacks to make everyday cooking easier. Baking mini frittatas in muffin tins is one of our favourite tricks. The basic process is so simple – just whisk eggs and milk, pour into muffin tins and bake – and the addition of roasted roots takes it even further, making it into a genuine meal. Adding a spoonful of pesto to the egg mixture complements the roasted root vegetables, too. When the muffins come out from the oven they are usually all puffy and glorious but it's normal for them to shrink slightly as they cool.

9 free-range eggs
120 ml (4 fl oz/½ cup) plant-based
   milk of choice
sea salt and freshly ground black
   pepper
1 handful (25 g/¾ oz) spinach

250 g (8¾ oz/2 cups) Roasted Roots
   and Veg (page 35)
100 g (3½ oz) feta
2 tbsp Perfect Pesto (page 25)
   or store-bought pesto

Crack the eggs into a medium-sized mixing bowl and add the milk. Season to taste with salt and pepper and whisk until thoroughly combined.

Roughly chop the spinach and divide between the cups of the muffin tin along with the roasted roots and feta. Pour the egg mixture into each cup and tap the tin lightly to make sure the mixture finds is way down between the vegetables. Top each muffin with half a teaspoon of the pesto.

Bake for about 20 minutes or until golden and the egg mixture has set. Remove from the oven and set aside to cool slightly in the tin before transferring to a wire rack to cool completely, or devouring them while still warm.

Store the cooled muffins in an airtight container in the fridge. They will keep for a few days.

TIP:
For a nut-free alternative, replace the pine nuts in the pesto with pumpkin or sunflower seeds.

Spinach and Feta Quiche with Oat Crust

Serves 4

Prep + cook time:
1 hour + 30 minutes
for the pastry to rest

This quiche is inspired by the Turkish spinach and feta hand-pie, börek (similar to the Greek spanakopita). Instead of using filo pastry, we came up with a simple gluten-free pie crust made with oats and almond flour. The quiche is full of flavour and rich but not too heavy. It is the perfect dish to take to a potluck or picnic since it is just as good cold as it is hot.

We always keep the crust the same but tend to change the filling slightly every time. Sometimes we add broccoli, as it is our daughter's favourite veg, and we also make it with various cheeses.

We recommend serving it with a simple tomato salad as the fresh tomatoes balance the richness of the quiche perfectly. This makes a picnic sized pie (20 cm/8 inches) but you can always double the recipe and bake it in a larger dish if you are cooking for a crowd.

PASTRY
65 g (2 oz/½ heaping cup) rolled oats (certified gluten-free)
50 g (1¾ oz/½ cup) almond or hazelnut flour
2 tbsp arrowroot (or potato starch)
½ tsp sea salt
3 tbsp virgin coconut oil, solidified, or 50 g (1¾ oz) butter, cubed and chilled
2 tbsp ice-cold filtered water

FILLING
2 tbsp extra-virgin olive oil
4 spring onions (scallions), trimmed
2 cloves of garlic, peeled
1 tsp dried oregano
½ tsp chilli flakes
100 g (3½ oz/2 cups) baby spinach or regular spinach, stems removed

FILLING (cont.)
sea salt and freshly ground black pepper
3 free-range eggs
60 ml (2 fl oz/¼ cup) plant-based milk of choice
½ tsp freshly grated nutmeg
150 g (5¼ oz) feta

CHERRY TOMATO SALAD
1 clove of garlic, peeled
3 tbsp extra-virgin olive oil
1 tbsp lemon juice
1 tsp balsamic vinegar
1 tsp wholegrain mustard
1 tsp runny honey
sea salt and freshly ground black pepper
20 cherry tomatoes
4 sprigs fresh thyme, leaves picked

continues overleaf

To make the pastry, place the oats in a food processor and blend until the texture resembles coarse flour. Transfer to a medium-sized mixing bowl, add the rest of the dry ingredients and stir until combined. Using your hands, rub the oil into the dry ingredients until the texture resembles breadcrumbs. Add the water, a tablespoon at a time, to bind all of the ingredients together. Knead the dough slightly, then shape it into a ball. Wrap in cling film (plastic wrap) and set aside in the fridge to rest for at least 30 minutes.

Preheat the oven to 180°C (350°F/Gas mark 4) and grease a 20 cm (8 inch) round fluted quiche dish or tart tin (ideally with a removable base). Unwrap the chilled dough, place it in the dish or tin and press it out evenly to cover the base and sides, making sure that it's flush with the edges of the dish. Prick the pastry base with a fork and bake blind for about 10 minutes or until the pastry is firm and slightly golden. Remove from the oven, set aside and reduce the oven temperature to 170°C (340°F/Gas mark 3½).

Meanwhile, prepare the filling. Heat the oil in a large frying pan (skillet) on a medium-low heat. Finely chop the spring onions and garlic, add them to the pan along with the oregano and chilli flakes and sauté for about 5 minutes or until the spring onions have softened. Remove from the heat, stir through the spinach while the onion mixture is still warm so that it wilts, season to taste with salt and pepper and set aside. Crack the eggs into a medium-sized mixing bowl, add the milk and nutmeg, and whisk until combined. Crumble in the feta, add the vegetables and stir until combined.

Pour the filling mixture into the pastry case and bake for about 30 minutes or until the filling is firm and golden. Remove from the oven and set aside to cool slightly, before removing from the tin and slicing.

While the quiche is baking, prepare the cherry tomato salad. To make the dressing, finely chop the garlic and add it to a medium-sized mixing bowl along with the rest of the wet ingredients. Season to taste with salt and pepper and whisk until combined. Cut the cherry tomatoes in half, add them to the mixing bowl along with the thyme and gently toss until well coated in the dressing.

Serve the quiche slightly warm accompanied by the tomato salad.

During the Week

If there is one thing I have learnt during my years working as an art director at interiors magazines, it is that a kitchen isn't complete without a large chalkboard scribbled with shopping lists or artfully scrawled clichés. I write that with a tiny bit of irony. My personal experience is that these chalkboards usually just end up being filled with kids' clutter and whenever we do list a missing ingredient on it, we tend to forget to buy it. But recently we have actually started using that pretty little vintage chalkboard of ours, to write weekly meal plans on it together with our daughter. We have found that involving Elsa in the planning really helps her get excited about the food that is being served throughout the week. And that often also leads to her helping out in the kitchen. We try to keep the menu varied but simple. This is how a week's meals in our house might look:

> *Monday*: A pasta dish (pages 92, 115 or 144)
> *Tuesday*: A curry or a soup with quinoa on the side (pages 138 or 143)
> *Wednesday*: A tray of oven-roasted vegetables and halloumi (page 116)
> *Thursday*: A stir-fry (using the leftover quinoa from Tuesday) (page 130)
> *Friday:* Crêpes with a variety of fillings (using whatever is left from the week) (page 127)

That also pretty much sums up the type of recipes we have in this chapter. It's a collection of simple and comforting dishes that provides you with a variety of flavours and methods without too much effort.

We have also included our #GKS Bowls (page 111) which we often make for lunch. At first glance they might just seem like random food tucked into a bowl, but there is actually a thought and method behind them to get a balanced mix of ingredients, texture and nutrients. *David*

#GKS Bowl – Four Seasonal Veggie Bowls

Each recipe:
Serves 1

This is how we create the lunch and dinner bowls that we have been sharing on social media over the years. Obviously, nourishing bowls like these can contain a wild mix of ingredients, but we try to make sure that we cover different ingredient types – a protein source or grain, healthy fats, baked veggies, raw veggies and raw fruit, leafy greens, dipping sauces and crunchy toppings – for a delicious and well-balanced bowl. We use many of the recipes from the Fridge Favourites chapter (pages 21–41) as the bases for these bowls, then add fresh, seasonal produce that we pick up from the store on our way home from work. As seasons, produce and availability vary between countries, don't feel you have to follow the recipes to the letter, but instead use them as a template and freestyle with the best vegetables and fruit you can find.

Spring

cooked Quick Quinoa (page 31)
    mixed with Perfect Pesto (page 25)
oven-roasted whole baby carrots*
steamed or blanched or fresh peas
shaved asparagus**
shaved raw radish**
lettuce leaves
cubed ripe pear
herbs

TO SERVE
toasted sunflower seeds
sea salt and freshly ground black
    pepper
extra-virgin olive oil

Summer

cooked Lazy Lentils (page 36)
grilled or sautéed sliced green
    and yellow courgette (zucchini)*
shaved raw fennel and fennel fronds**
halved heirloom tomatoes
baby spinach leaves
halved fresh strawberries
grilled or pan-fried sliced halloumi

TO SERVE
ajvar (roasted red pepper) sauce
roughly chopped fresh mint leaves
roughly chopped toasted almonds
sea salt and freshly ground black
    pepper
extra-virgin olive oil

* Drizzle the vegetables with extra-virgin olive oil, season to taste with sea salt and freshly ground black pepper and toss until well coated before grilling, sautéing or roasting at 200°C (400°F/ Gas mark 6) for 20–30 minutes or until tender and golden.

** Drizzle the vegetables or leafy greens with extra-virgin olive oil, freshly squeezed lemon juice, season to taste with salt and pepper and toss until well coated.

Autumn

cooked millet

oven-roasted cubed aubergine
(eggplant)*

shaved raw Chioggia beetroot (beet)**

kale leaves, stems removed**

fresh blueberries

halved soft-boiled free-range egg
sprinkled with sumac, smoked
paprika or za'atar

TO SERVE

Heavenly Hummus (page 26)

roughly chopped fresh flat-leaf
parsley leaves

toasted pumpkin seeds

sea salt and freshly ground black
pepper

extra-virgin olive oil

Winter

cooked cannellini beans or beans
of choice

Roasted Roots and Veg (page 35)

spiralized or shaved raw courgette
(zucchini)**

Golden Sauerkraut (page 205)

lettuce leaves

sliced apple

TO SERVE

full-fat plain unsweetened yoghurt
of choice

Savoury Granola (page 200)

sea salt and freshly ground black
pepper

extra-virgin olive oil

Toss the millet or beans with some oil or dipping sauce. Arrange the quinoa, lentils, millet or beans in a bowl alongside the cooked, raw (and fermented, if using) vegetables, leafy greens, fruit, and source of protein. Serve topped with a dollop of your chosen sauce (pesto, ajvar, hummus or yoghurt), a scattering of herbs (if using), a sprinkling of the seeds or nuts and seasoning, and a drizzle of the oil.

Mushroom, Goat's Cheese, Pear and Walnut Fettuccine

Serves 4

Prep + cook time:
20 minutes

TIPS:
We often use bean fettuccine made from 100% organic mung bean flour (or soy bean flour). There are different varieties available in most well-stocked supermarkets or health food stores, so pick your favourite.

For a nut-free alternative, replace the walnuts with pumpkin seeds or sunflower seeds.

For a vegan alternative, replace the goat's cheese with a vegan soft cheese, and the pecorino with a vegan hard cheese.

This is the pasta version of a goat's cheese, pear and walnut salad that we have been making for years. It's simplicity itself, using only a handful of delicious ingredients. We often choose pasta made from dried bean flour, which adds protein to the dish that normally is only carb-heavy.

2 tbsp butter or extra-virgin olive oil
2 cloves of garlic, peeled
2 sprigs fresh rosemary, leaves picked
20 leaves fresh sage
500 g (1 lb) mixed mushrooms of choice, cleaned
50 g (1¾ oz/1 cup) baby spinach or regular spinach, stems removed
200 g (7 oz) soft goat's (chèvre) cheese, crumbled
sea salt and freshly ground black pepper

TO SERVE
bean, buckwheat or regular fettuccine (enough for 4 servings)
firm but ripe pear
freshly grated pecorino, Grana Padano or Parmigiano Reggiano
roughly chopped toasted walnuts
sea salt and freshly ground black pepper
cold-pressed extra-virgin olive oil or walnut oil
balsamic vinegar

Bring a large pan of water to the boil. Add a generous pinch of salt and the fettuccine, stir, and cook until al dente (according to the packet instructions).

Meanwhile, heat the butter or oil in a large frying pan (skillet) on a medium-low heat. Finely chop the garlic, rosemary and sage, add them to the pan and sauté for a minute or so, or until fragrant.

Thinly slice the mushrooms, add them to the pan and sauté on a medium-high heat (without stirring) for about 5 minutes, or until golden. Turn them over and sauté for a further 5 minutes or until golden and tender. Remove from the heat, stir through the spinach and goat's cheese until the spinach has wilted and the cheese has melted, then season to taste with salt and pepper. You may need to add some water (preferably pasta water) to loosen the sauce if it's too dry.

Fold the cooked fettuccine through the sauce and serve topped with some pear slices, a sprinkling of pecorino, walnuts, seasoning and a drizzle of oil and vinegar.

Mediterranean Tray-bake with Halloumi Chunks

Serves 4

Prep + cook time:
50 minutes

Preparing a full meal on a single tray and then just letting the oven handle all of the cooking is (or should be) every family's favourite easy-cooking solution. It allows us to spend more time with each other and still have a delicious and wholesome meal on the table in time for dinner (and little to wash up). This is one of our (and our kids') favourite versions, with mixed vegetables, Mediterranean flavours and squeaky halloumi chunks. Serve with a simple green salad on the side.

400 g (14 oz) baby potatoes, scrubbed
4 carrots, tops removed and scrubbed
2 red (bell) peppers, core and seeds removed
1 courgette (zucchini), topped and tailed
1 garlic bulb
1 lemon, washed
2 sprigs fresh rosemary
4 tbsp extra-virgin olive oil
sea salt and freshly ground black pepper

250 g (8¾ oz) halloumi
12 black Kalamata olives, drained and pitted

TO SERVE
rocket (arugula) or mesclun
toasted pine nuts
sea salt and freshly ground black pepper
extra-virgin olive oil
balsamic vinegar

Preheat the oven to 200°C (400°F/Gas mark 6) and line a baking tray with parchment paper.

Cut the potatoes, carrots, peppers and courgette into bite-sized pieces, cut the garlic in half crosswise and cut the lemon into thin wedges. Transfer to the baking tray and add the rosemary. Drizzle over the oil, season to taste with salt and pepper and toss until well coated. Bake for 25–30 minutes or until the vegetables are almost tender.

Break up the halloumi into bite-sized pieces and scatter it over the vegetables along with the olives. Change the oven mode to grill, increase the temperature and grill the halloumi, olives and vegetables for 5–10 minutes or until the halloumi is soft and golden and the vegetables are tender and golden.

Serve topped with a handful of rocket, a sprinkling of pine nuts and seasoning and a drizzle of oil and vinegar.

TIPS:
For a nut-free alternative, replace the pine nuts with pumpkin seeds or sunflower seeds.

For a vegan alternative, leave out the halloumi or replace it with marinated tofu or tempeh.

Daily Dhal

Serves 6

Prep + cook time:
50 minutes

This dhal was one of the first recipes I learnt to cook after moving into my own flat, and became something I made almost on a daily basis (alternated with quick-cooked pasta and tomato sauce that all 18-year-old boys swear by). A friend born in Bangladesh taught me the recipe. I still remember being shocked by the insane amounts of spices he used and his secret trick to round off the flavour of the spices (stir an enormous chunk of butter into the warm soup before serving). My recipe has a more westernised dosage of spices and I have left out the butter to keep it vegan. If you are not vegan, however, I have to admit that one or two tablespoons of butter or ghee rounds off the flavours perfectly!

Fifteen years in, this is still a soup that we make very often. It is one of the most comforting meals we know – it tastes like a big hug – and the kids love it as well. *David*

2 tbsp virgin coconut oil
1 onion, peeled
3 cloves of garlic, peeled
1 tbsp fresh ginger, grated
1 tbsp curry powder
1 tsp ground turmeric
¼–½ tsp chilli powder
3 low-starch or waxy potatoes, peeled
2 carrots, tops removed and peeled
200 g (7 oz/1 cup) red lentils, rinsed
1 litre (32 fl oz/4 cups) vegetable stock

sea salt
3 tomatoes

TO SERVE
1 apple
toasted hazelnuts, coarsely chopped
sea salt and freshly ground black
    pepper
roughly chopped fresh coriander
    (cilantro) leaves

VARIATIONS:
Stir through a handful of spinach leaves towards the last minute of cooking.

Add 1 tsp of ground cumin and 1 tsp of mustard seeds along with the other spices for a richer flavour.

TIP:
For a nut-free alternative, replace the hazelnuts with toasted pumpkin seeds.

Heat the oil in a large saucepan on a medium-low heat. Finely chop the onion and garlic, add them to the pan along with the ginger and spices, and sauté for about 10 minutes or until the onion begins to soften.

Meanwhile, cut the potatoes and carrots into small cubes. Add them to the pan and sauté for a further 5 minutes. Add the lentils and stock to the pan and season to taste with salt. Bring to the boil, reduce the heat and simmer for about 30 minutes or until the lentils are cooked, stirring from time to time so the dhal doesn't burn. In the last 5 minutes of cooking, finely dice and stir through the tomatoes.

Core the apple and cut it into thin sticks. Serve the dhal topped with a sprinkling of the apple sticks, hazelnuts, seasoning and coriander.

Warm Black Beans and Greens with Avo and Za'atar

Serves 2

Prep + cook time:
15 minutes

We often turn to this for lunch, when time is short and we crave something warm and comforting with minimal effort. It comes together within the first five songs (15 minutes) of Bon Iver's *For Emma* album (which is what we most often listen to while we cook) and feels both healthy and delicious. The broccoli should still have some bite, and the spinach be barely wilted, for the nicest texture. It can be served with a poached egg as well, but the 'avo-egg' quenelle makes it perfect for vegans and adds good fat to the dish.

2 tbsp extra-virgin olive oil
1 onion, peeled
½ broccoli, head and stalk
10 cherry tomatoes
100 g (3½ oz/2 cups) baby spinach
    or regular spinach, stems removed
1 × 400 g (14 oz) tin black beans,*
    drained and rinsed
sea salt and freshly ground black
    pepper

AVOCADO QUENELLES
1 ripe avocado, stone removed and
    flesh scooped out
juice of 1 lime

TO SERVE
Za'atar (page 202)
sea salt and freshly ground black
    pepper
extra-virgin olive oil

Heat the oil in a large frying pan (skillet) on a medium-low heat. Roughly chop the onion, add it to the pan and sauté for about 5 minutes or until the onion has softened. Cut the broccoli into small florets and trim and finely slice the stalk. Add the florets and stalk to the pan and sauté for a further 5 minutes. Halve the tomatoes and add them to the pan along with the spinach. Once the spinach has wilted, stir through the beans and season to taste with salt and pepper. Remove from the heat, cover and set aside.

To prepare the avocado quenelles, mash the avocado in a bowl with a fork until smooth and stir through the lime juice. Dip two spoons into hot water and shake off the excess water. Take a generous scoop of the mashed avocado, and pass the mixture repeatedly between the spoons, turning and smoothing each side until a neat quenelle is formed.

Serve the black beans and greens warm in bowls, topped with avocado quenelles, a sprinkling of za'atar and seasoning and a drizzle of oil.

* Or use 200 g (7 oz/1½ cups) cooked black beans.

TIP:
If you can't find za'atar or sumac, add a squeeze of lime, some toasted sesame seeds, dried thyme and cumin instead.

Baked Fennel, Watermelon and Goat's Cheese Summer Salad

Serves 4

Prep + cook time:
45 minutes

One of the most important traits of a good salad is its texture. You want both the creamy and the crunchy, the large leaves and the small nutty bits, vegetables that are roasted until soft and tender mixed with thinly shaved raw ones. And, finally, something fresh and fruity that splashes on your teeth as you bite into it. This salad has all that – it is absolute heaven on hot summer days.

1 fennel bulb, stalks removed
2 tbsp extra-virgin olive oil
sea salt and freshly ground black pepper
¼ small watermelon, rind and seeds removed
4 heirloom tomatoes, tops removed
1 raw beetroot (beet), trimmed, tops removed and peeled
1 carrot, tops removed and peeled
1 red apple, cored
½ cucumber, topped and tailed
1 small head cosmopolitan, romaine or Cos lettuce, stump removed
150 g (5¼ oz/1 cup) cooked Quick Quinoa (page 31)

1 tbsp extra-virgin olive oil
150 g (5¼ oz) soft goat's (chèvre) cheese, sliced

YOGHURT DRESSING
8 fresh basil leaves, finely chopped
120 ml (4 fl oz/½ cup) full-fat unsweetened plain yoghurt
juice and zest of ½ unwaxed lemon
sea salt and freshly ground black pepper

TO SERVE
roughly chopped toasted walnuts
torn fresh basil leaves
extra-virgin olive oil

Preheat the oven to 200°C (400°F/Gas mark 6) and line a baking tray with parchment paper.

Cut the fennel into wedges, toss with the oil, season to taste with salt and pepper and transfer to the baking tray. Bake for 25–30 minutes or until tender and caramelised. Remove from the oven and set aside to cool. Stir together the ingredients for the dressing in a small mixing bowl. Season to taste and set aside.

To assemble the salad, cut the watermelon and tomatoes into bite-sized pieces, shave the beetroot and carrot lengthwise with a mandoline or potato peeler and thinly slice the apple and cucumber. Tear the lettuce leaves into large pieces and toss with the quinoa and oil, then place on a serving dish. Arrange the all the vegetables, fruit and goat's cheese on top. Serve with the yoghurt dressing, a scattering of walnuts and basil and a drizzle of oil.

TIPS:
For a nut-free alternative, replace the walnuts with pumpkin seeds or sunflower seeds.

For a vegan alternative, replace the goat's cheese with a vegan soft cheese and the yoghurt with a plant-based yoghurt.

Beetroot and Feta Patties

Makes 6–8 patties

Prep + cook time:
50 minutes

These red, juicy patties almost look like meat, but they are so much better. Not only are they moist and flavourful but they have a beautiful texture, too. Burgers are, of course, ideal inside a bun, but we wanted to show you another way to serve them. Here, we serve them in lettuce leaf cups, paired with a slaw and some avocado and toasted seeds. The leaf can be used as a wrapper, so you can eat it with your hands, or as a salad in the bowl.

BEETROOT PATTIES
3–4 (350 g/12¼ oz) raw beetroots (beets), peeled
10 g/⅓ oz fresh basil, leaves picked
1 small onion, peeled
2 cloves of garlic, peeled
150 g (5¼ oz/1½ cups) rolled oats
2 tbsp extra-virgin olive oil
2 free-range eggs
200 g (7 oz) feta or organic firm tofu, drained and cubed
1 tsp sea salt
½ tsp freshly ground black pepper
extra-virgin olive oil or coconut oil (to fry)

CABBAGE SLAW
120 ml (4 fl oz/½ cup) full-fat plain unsweetened yoghurt
1 tbsp organic unfiltered apple cider vinegar
1 tsp runny honey or pure maple syrup
sea salt and freshly ground black pepper
½ white cabbage, trimmed
2 carrots, tops removed and peeled

TO SERVE
large lettuce leaves
sliced ripe avocado
sprouts
seeds

Alternatively, bake the patties in the oven at 200°C (400°F/ Gas mark 6) for 20 minutes, flip and bake for a further 5–10 minutes or until golden on both sides. Or put them on the grill.

TIP:
Substitute feta for tofu and lemon for a dairy-free version.

Coarsely grate the beetroots, roughly chop the basil, finely chop the onion and garlic and place in a large mixing bowl with the oats and oil. Crack in the eggs, crumble in the feta, season to taste and mix to combine. Cover and put in the fridge for at least 30 minutes or until the oats have absorbed the liquid.

Meanwhile, prepare the slaw. Place the yoghurt, vinegar and honey in a mixing bowl, season to taste and mix. Grate or shred the cabbage and carrots and add them to the bowl. Stir to combine and set aside.

Using your hands, shape the mixture into 6–8 large patties. Heat 1 tablespoon of oil in a large non-stick frying pan (skillet) on a medium-high heat. Fry the patties for a few minutes or until the base is golden. Carefully flip with a spatula and fry the other side.* Serve in bowls with lettuce, avocado, slaw, sprouts and seeds.

Spinach Crêpes with Creamy Chickpeas and Mushrooms

Out of all the recipes in this book, this is, without a doubt, the most popular one in our home. We have been making green crêpes for years and it's just so nice to have a quick backup that we know everyone likes. The spinach and basil in the batter add colour and flavour, and also make them healthier. We serve them with different fillings every time, depending on what we have available. Our chickpea (garbanzo bean) filling is always a good option, and simple fried mushrooms are a favourite too We also love cottage cheese or feta, Roasted Roots and Veg (page 35) and the Heavenly Hummus (page 26). And we always eat the last crepe with a simple, lightly sweetened berry compote.

SPINACH CRÊPES
1 quantity Rice Crêpe Batter (page 32)
50 g (1¾ oz/1 cup) baby spinach or regular spinach, stems removed, or frozen spinach (thawed)
12 fresh basil leaves
virgin coconut oil or butter, to fry

CREAMY CHICKPEAS
3 tbsp extra-virgin olive oil
3 tbsp tahini
juice of 1 lemon
1 tsp runny honey or pure maple syrup
sea salt and freshly ground black pepper
2 small red apples, cored
2 × 400 g (14 oz) tins chickpeas (garbanzo beans),* drained and rinsed

SAUTÉED MUSHROOMS
2 tbsp extra-virgin olive oil, virgin coconut oil or butter
500 g (1 lb) mixed mushrooms, cleaned
2 garlic of cloves, peeled
2 tsp fresh thyme leaves
sea salt and freshly ground black pepper

TO SERVE
toasted sunflower seeds
fresh basil leaves
fresh sprouts
sea salt and freshly ground black pepper
extra-virgin olive oil

* Or 500 g (1 lb/2 cups) cooked chickpeas (garbanzo beans) (page 26).

continues overleaf

Place the crêpe batter in a blender or food processor, add the spinach and basil, and blend until completely smooth and green.

To prepare the creamy chickpeas, place the oil, tahini, lemon juice and honey or maple syrup in a medium-sized serving bowl, season to taste with salt and pepper and whisk until combined. Grate or dice the apples, transfer to the bowl along with the chickpeas, mix until well coated in the dressing and set aside.

To prepare the sautéed mushrooms, heat the oil in a large frying pan (skillet) on a medium-high heat. Finely slice the mushrooms and finely chop the garlic. Add them to the pan along with the thyme, season to taste with salt and pepper, and sauté (without stirring) for about 5 minutes or until golden. Turn them over and sauté for a further 5 minutes or until tender and golden. Remove from the heat and set aside while you cook the crêpes.

Heat a little oil in a 20 cm (8 inch) non-stick frying pan on a medium-high heat. Once hot, whisk the batter then ladle 80 ml (2½ fl oz/⅓ cup) into the pan, tilting the pan to spread and evenly distribute the batter. Fry for 1–2 minutes or until small bubbles form on the surface and the base is golden. Carefully flip the crêpe with a spatula and fry the other side for a further 1–2 minutes or until cooked and golden. Transfer to a plate and repeat with the rest of the batter (you may need to reduce the heat slightly after the first crêpe).

Top each crêpe with some chickpeas and mushrooms, a scattering of sunflower seeds, basil and sprouts, a sprinkling of seasoning and a drizzle of oil, then fold in half and serve.

Chanterelle, Quinoa and Tofu Stir-fry

Serves 4

Prep + cook time:
25 minutes

Whenever we have half a bag of this and some leftovers of that, we bring out the frying pan (skillet) and stir-fry our way to dinner. Cooked rice is a common base but since we more often have a jar of quinoa in the fridge, we usually go for that.

In Scandinavia we are fortunate enough to have chanterelles, porcini and funnel chanterelles available in most forests during the autumn. It's free food! Unfortunately, both David and I are terrible at foraging. We either get lost in the forest or constantly look in the wrong areas and end up with only just enough mushrooms to cover a sandwich or fill-out a stir-fry. That's how this recipe was born. With too few chanterelles for a mushroom stew, and some leftover quinoa and tofu in the fridge, we improvised and came up with this. *Luise*

1 tbsp extra-virgin olive oil or butter
1 onion, peeled
2 cloves of garlic, peeled
1 tsp fresh ginger, grated
1 fennel bulb, stalks removed, fronds set aside for garnish
1 courgette (zucchini), topped and tailed
400 g (14 oz) organic firm tofu, drained
300 g (10½ oz) chanterelles or mushrooms of choice, cleaned
300 g (10½ oz/2 cups) cooked Quick Quinoa (page 31) or cooked rice or millet

sea salt and freshly ground black pepper
2 handfuls (60 g/2 oz) baby spinach

TO SERVE
raw or blanched corn cob kernels
crumbled feta
1 large handful roughly chopped fresh fennel fronds and/or flat-leaf parsley leaves
sea salt and freshly ground black pepper
lime juice
olive oil

TIPS:
For a vegan alternative, leave out the feta and add 1 tsp of nutritional yeast with the tofu.

Sweet and fresh corn cobs can be pleasantly juicy raw, but some types need to be blanched first to soften up.

Heat the oil or butter in a large frying pan (skillet) on a medium heat. Finely chop the onion and garlic, add them to the pan together with the ginger, and sauté for about 5 minutes or until the onion begins to soften. Roughly chop the fennel and courgette and cut the tofu into cubes. Add the vegetables and tofu to the pan and sauté for a further 5 minutes.

Slice the mushrooms into strips, add to the pan and sauté until all of the vegetables are tender. Stir through the quinoa and let it fry for 2–3 minutes. Season to taste with salt and pepper, remove from the heat and stir through the spinach.

Serve topped with a sprinkling of corn kernels, feta, herbs and seasoning and a generous squeeze of lime juice and a drizzle of olive oil.

Flatbread Pizzette

Serves 4

Prep + cook time:
20 minutes

When time is short and hunger is imminent, this little shortcut recipe will give you dinner on the table really quickly. We just slather pesto on top of slices of our Rainbow Flatbread (page 38), cover them with thinly sliced veggies (cheese, if preferred) and herbs, then roast or grill on a high heat until crispy. We have made two different combinations – one with mushroom and rocket (arugula), and one with a Caprese-inspired topping – but just like ordinary pizzas, a heap of other toppings can be added. Just be sure to slice hard vegetables thinly so they will be baked in the short time. Our Big-batch Tomato Sauce (page 22) can be used instead of pesto.

16 slices Rainbow Flatbreads
    (page 38) or flatbreads of choice
1 quantity Perfect Pesto (page 25)
    or store-bought
2 portobello mushrooms or 4 cremini
    mushrooms, cleaned
16 heirloom cherry tomatoes
125 g (4½ oz) buffalo mozzarella
2 tbsp extra-virgin olive oil

2 tsp dried herbs of choice
    (e.g. thyme, basil or oregano)
sea salt and freshly ground black
    pepper

TO SERVE
fresh thyme leaves or torn fresh basil
    leaves
rocket (arugula) leaves

Preheat the oven to 250°C (500°F/Gas mark 8) and line a baking tray with parchment paper.

Place the flatbreads on the tray and spread them with the pesto. Thinly slice the mushrooms and tomatoes and arrange separately on top of the flatbreads. Break the mozzarella into small pieces and tuck them in between or on top of the tomatoes. Brush the toppings with the oil, sprinkle over the herbs and season to taste with salt and pepper.

Bake for about 10 minutes or until crispy and golden. Remove from the oven and serve the tomato pizzette topped with a sprinkling of fresh herbs and the mushroom pizzette with a scattering of rocket.

TIP:
For a vegan alternative, simply leave out the mozzarella and make the vegan version of our Perfect Pesto (page 25).

Fifty Shades of Greens

Serves 4

Prep + cook time:
35 minutes

The original version of this recipe was created a decade ago, in the tiny apartment in Rome that was my temporary home. It was one of the first dishes I cooked for Luise and I like to think that it was then and there that she fell for me (and not watching my drunk feet trying to seduce her on the dance floor a week earlier). The original version didn't include quite as many green vegetables – it was made with double (heavy) cream and served with pasta – but the essence was the same: green, creamy and delicious.

You can use frozen broccoli and spinach instead of fresh, swap peas for beans and use olives instead of capers. If you don't fancy coconut milk or cream, use ordinary cream, Greek yoghurt (added right at the end) or a vegan alternative. Serve with cooked quinoa, millet, rice or pasta of choice. *David*

3 tbsp virgin coconut oil or extra-virgin olive oil
1 onion, peeled
2 cloves of garlic, peeled
8 sprigs fresh thyme, leaves picked, or 1 tsp dried thyme
1 broccoli, head and stalk
1 courgette (zucchini)
3 tbsp capers, plus brine
120 ml (4 fl oz/½ cup) white wine
190 g (6¾ oz/1½ cups) frozen green peas

100 g (3½ oz/2 cups) spinach
1 × 400 g (14 oz) tin full-fat coconut cream or milk
250 ml (8 fl oz/1 cup) vegetable stock
sea salt and freshly ground black pepper
zest and juice of ½ unwaxed lemon

TO SERVE
Quick Quinoa (page 31) or cooked grain or pasta of choice
roughly chopped flat-leaf parsley

Heat the oil in a large saucepan on a medium-low heat. Finely chop the onion, garlic and thyme, transfer to the pan and sauté for about 10 minutes or until the onion begins to soften. Cut the broccoli into small florets, trim and slice the stalk and cut the courgette into half circles. Add the vegetables to the pan along with the capers and brine and sauté for a further 5 minutes, then add the wine.

Once the alcohol has evaporated, add the peas, spinach coconut cream and stock and season. Bring to the boil then reduce the heat and simmer until the vegetables are tender and the sauce has thickened, stirring from time to time so the sauce doesn't burn. Remove from the heat and stir through the lemon zest and juice. Serve with quinoa, topped with a sprinkling of parsley.

Roasted Butternut Squash Soup with Goat's Cheese Yoghurt

Serves 4

Prep + cook time:
50 minutes

Butternut squash or pumpkin is one of the trickiest vegetables to peel and with this method you don't have to peel it at all. The butternut is simply halved then roasted, so its soft flesh can be scooped with a spoon straight into a blender together with a few other simple ingredients. So easy and delicious too!

You can also make this soup using our Pumpkin Purée on page 28. Just skip the first part of the recipe, add the purée to the blender with the rest of the ingredients and heat the soup in a saucepan before serving.

910 g (2 lb) butternut squash or 500 g (1 lb/2 cups) Pumpkin Purée (page 28)
250–500 ml (8–16 fl oz/1–2 cups) hot vegetable stock or water
1 × 400 g (14 oz) tin coconut milk
1 tbsp organic unfiltered apple cider vinegar
1 tsp grated ginger
1 sprig fresh rosemary, leaves picked
sea salt and freshly ground black pepper

GOAT'S CHEESE YOGHURT
150 g (5¼ oz) soft goat's (chèvre) cheese
60 ml (2 fl oz/¼ cup) full-fat plain unsweetened yoghurt

TO SERVE
rosemary leaves
sea salt and freshly ground black pepper
extra-virgin olive oil

Preheat the oven to 200°C (400°F/Gas mark 6) and line a baking tray with parchment paper.

Cut the butternut squash in half lengthwise and remove the seeds with a spoon. Place both halves on the baking tray, cut side down, and bake for 30–45 minutes or until the flesh is tender and the skin is golden and bubbly.

To make the goat's cheese yoghurt, place the goat's cheese in a mixing bowl, mash with a fork then add the yoghurt. Whisk until fully combined and set aside.

Remove the squash from the oven and set aside to cool slightly, then spoon out the flesh, add it to a large saucepan or a food processor along with the rest of the ingredients (start with 250 ml/8 fl oz/1 cup vegetable stock or water) and season to taste with salt and pepper. Using an immersion (hand) blender or food processor, blend until smooth, adding extra stock, if desired.

Serve topped with a swirl of goat's cheese yoghurt, seeds, rosemary and some seasoning, and a drizzle of oil.

TIP:
For a vegan alternative, replace the goat's cheese with a vegan soft cheese and the yoghurt with coconut yoghurt.

Courgette, Fennel and Turmeric Soup

Serves 4

Prep + cook time:
40 minutes

This is a soup for days when raindrops hit our windows, summer is fading away and autumn is knocking on our door. This is a light and brothy bowl with earthy turmeric tones, a whisper of anise from the fennel, tanginess from lime and roundness from a splash of wine, and a subtle kick from ginger and chilli. We serve it ladled over quinoa or rice and add toppings generously.

1 tbsp extra-virgin olive oil
1 onion, peeled
2 cloves of garlic, peeled
1 tbsp peeled and grated fresh
    turmeric, or ½ tbsp ground
    turmeric
1 tbsp peeled and grated fresh ginger
¼–½ tsp chilli flakes
1 fennel bulb, stalks removed, fronds
    set aside
2 courgettes (zucchinis)
60 ml (2 fl oz/¼ cup) white wine
1 litre (32 fl oz/4 cups) vegetable stock
zest and juice of 1 lime
sea salt and freshly ground black
    pepper

TO SERVE
Quick Quinoa (page 31) or cooked
    millet or brown rice
full-fat plain unsweetened yoghurt
    or cottage cheese
pumpkin seeds, toasted
roughly chopped flat-leaf parsley
    leaves
sea salt and freshly ground black
    pepper
extra-virgin olive oil

VARIATIONS:
This can be served with dumplings or fried courgette (zucchini) flowers if you want to take it from a simple weekday soup to a moreish weekend version.

Try the goat's cheese yoghurt on page 137 for a more distinct flavour twist.

TIP:
For a vegan alternative, replace the yoghurt with a plant-based yoghurt such as coconut or soy.

Heat the oil in a large saucepan on a medium-low heat. Roughly chop the onion and finely chop the garlic, then add them to the pan along with the spices and sauté for about 5 minutes or until the onion begins to soften.

Roughly chop the fennel and courgettes, add them to the pan and sauté for a further 5 minutes or until the onion has softened, then add the wine. Once the alcohol has evaporated, add the stock and lime zest and season to taste. Bring to the boil, then simmer for about 15 minutes or until the vegetables are tender, stirring from time to time so the soup doesn't burn on the base of the pan.

Remove from the heat, roughly chop the fennel fronds and stir them through the soup with the lime juice. Serve on top of quinoa, millet or rice, topped with a dollop of yoghurt or cottage cheese, a sprinkling of seeds, parsley and seasoning and a drizzle of oil.

Roasted Root and Rye Waffle Toastie

Serves 2

Prep + cook time:
15 minutes

One Christmas, many years ago, I was given a little electric sandwich maker in the shape of a dog. I've used it a handful of times and always thought it was not only indescribably ugly but also impractical: as it is made for toast bread. We use everything from small, thick rye bread slices to huge artisanal sourdough bread slices and they don't really fit in the sandwich dog. I have instead come to realise that our waffle iron does a much better job. It can handle all sizes of bread and it leaves a nice crusty waffle pattern on the bread. So waffle toasties have become a 'thing' in our home.

One of my favourite versions is this one with roots, mayo and Dijon mustard. Some days I add a slice of aged cheese for an even richer sandwich, and other days we skip the mayo for a vegan version. The sauerkraut can be swapped for pickled red onion or other lacto-fermented vegetables, or our Beetroot Spread (page 211). *David*

1½ tbsp mayonnaise
½ tbsp wholegrain or Dijon mustard
½ ripe avocado, stone removed and
    flesh scooped out
1 tbsp lemon juice
sea salt and freshly ground black
    pepper
4 slices sourdough rye bread

100 g (3½ oz/⅔ cup) Roasted Roots
    and Veg (page 35)
1 handful (25 g/¾ oz) baby spinach
    or regular spinach
2 tbsp Sauerkraut (pages 205–6)
    (optional)
2 tbsp extra-virgin olive oil

Preheat the waffle iron. Place the mayonnaise and mustard in a small bowl, mix until combined and set aside. Place the avocado flesh and lemon juice in a medium-sized bowl, season to taste with salt and pepper and mash with a fork until combined.

To assemble, spread the bottom slices of the bread with the mustard mayo and the top slices with the avocado mash. Arrange the roasted roots and spinach on top of the mustard mayo, followed by sauerkraut (if using). Cover with the top slices, brush the outside of each slice with the oil and toast for a few minutes or until golden and crispy.

Serve cut in half.

TIP:
For a vegan alternative, choose a vegan mayonnaise or omit it altogether.

No Recipe Coconut Curry

Serves 6

Prep + cook time:
40 minutes

This weeknight curry runs on repeat like an old record in our home. It is a simple and comforting recipe that everyone in our family loves. Most importantly, it's a recipe that we always have the ingredients for. And if we don't have everything, we just replace it with something else. Which is why we call it 'no-recipe': it rarely turns out the same way twice. There are plenty of ways to tweak it. We sometimes add mustard seeds, galangal or fresh lemongrass with the other spices if we have them to hand. Replace any of the vegetables with whatever is in season – pumpkin, courgette (zucchini), tomatoes or aubergine (eggplant) will all fit right in.

2 tbsp virgin coconut oil
    or ghee
1 onion, peeled
3 cloves of garlic, peeled
1 tsp fresh red chilli, seeded,
    or ½ tsp chilli flakes
2 tbsp peeled and grated fresh ginger
1 tbsp ground turmeric
3 dried curry leaves, torn
1 tsp ground coriander
1 tsp ground cumin
1 sweet potato, peeled
1 small broccoli, head and stalk
200 g (7 oz) organic firm tofu, drained

2 × 400 g (14 oz) tins coconut milk
sea salt and freshly ground black
    pepper
100 g (3½ oz/2 cups) spinach
juice of 1 lime

TO SERVE
500 g (1 lb/3 cups) Quick Quinoa (page
    31) or cooked brown basmati rice
cashew nuts, toasted
nigella seeds
1 large handful roughly chopped fresh
    coriander (cilantro) leaves
sea salt and freshly ground black
    pepper

Heat the oil or ghee in a large saucepan on a medium heat. Finely chop the onion, garlic and chilli and add them to the pan along with the ginger, turmeric, curry leaves, coriander and cumin. Sauté for 5 minutes until the onion begins to soften.

Meanwhile, cut the sweet potato into small cubes, cut the broccoli into florets, and trim and roughly chop the stalks. Add the vegetables to the pan and sauté for 10 minutes or until the onion has softened.

Cut the tofu into small cubes and add to the pan along with the coconut milk and season to taste. Bring to the boil, reduce the heat and simmer until the vegetables are tender, stirring occasionally. Add more water if it seems dry.

Remove from the heat and stir through the spinach and lime juice. Serve over quinoa or rice and top with cashew nuts, nigella seeds, coriander and seasoning.

TIP:
For a nut-free alternative, replace the cashew nuts with pumpkin seeds or sunflower seeds.

Penne al Pomodoro
with Vegan 'Tuna'

Serves 4

Prep + cook time:
20 minutes + 6 hours
for the sunflower seeds
to soak

By pulsing soaked sunflower seeds with salty capers, onion, oil, apple cider vinegar, lemon and nori sheets in a food processor, you actually get something that looks surprisingly similar to tinned tuna, with a crumbly, moist texture and a flavour that reminds us of salty seas and umami.

You can use the 'tuna' as a spread or in a salad (with the addition of celery and fresh herbs) but we like to add it to a tomato sauce and serve it with penne, creating a classic Italian peasant dish. The vegan 'tuna' adds a nice texture to the sauce and it improves the flavour, too. The kids love it! It is a simple recipe if you are on a budget and it is a tad more special than your basic pasta al pomodoro. So, go put your sunflower seeds in water and pretend they are a fish!

FOR THE VEGAN 'TUNA'
1 small red onion, peeled
150 g (5¼ oz/1 cup) sunflower seeds,
    soaked in filtered water for 6 hours,
    then strained and rinsed
1 raw nori sheet, crushed (or another
    sea vegetable or flavouring)
3 tbsp capers, plus brine
1 tbsp extra-virgin olive oil
1 tbsp lemon juice
1 tsp unfiltered apple cider vinegar
½ tsp sea salt

FOR THE SUGO AL POMODORO
120 ml (4 fl oz/½ cup) white wine
    or vegetable stock
½ quantity (1¼ litres/4½ cups)
    Big-batch Tomato Sauce
    (page 22)

TO SERVE
cooked wholegrain or gluten-free
    pasta of choice (e.g. penne)
caper berries, drained and rinsed
roughly chopped fresh parsley leaves
sea salt and freshly ground black
    pepper
extra-virgin olive oil

TIPS:
The 'tuna' can also be prepared in a medium-sized bowl with an immersion (hand) blender or by using a pestle and mortar.

It's important to soak the sunflower seeds to achieve the right texture, so don't skip that step.

Roughly chop the onion, transfer to a food processor, add the rest of the ingredients and pulse until the texture resembles that of tuna.

Place a large frying pan (skillet) on a medium-low heat, add the wine and the tomato sauce, bring to the boil, reduce the heat and add the 'tuna' (reserving a little bit for serving). Let it simmer for about 10 minutes, stirring occasionally so the sauce doesn't burn. Stir the sauce through the pasta. Serve topped with some caper berries, a sprinkling of parsley and some seasoning. Finish with a drizzle of oil.

Green Pea, Broccoli and Mint Soup with Puy Lentil Topping

Serves 4

Prep + cook time:
45 minutes

We are just going to quote our recipe tester, Nic, on this one. Her words, not ours: 'This soup is absolutely DELICIOUS!!! Made it several times! It's so flavoursome (love the combo of the peas and mint), so smooth and creamy thanks to that coconut milk, yet has lots of body from the broccoli, super-nutritious with all those gorgeous green veggies and has the best textural toppings! And what a bonus the fact that it's super easy, quick and cheap to make!!! Next-level good!!!'
Enjoy!

1 tbsp virgin coconut oil
1 onion, peeled
2 cloves of garlic, peeled
2 tbsp peeled and grated fresh ginger
250 g (8¾ oz/2 cups) frozen green peas
250 g (8¾ oz/2 cups) fresh broccoli, stalks included, roughly chopped (or frozen broccoli florets)
500 ml (16 fl oz/2 cups) vegetable stock
sea salt and freshly ground black pepper
1 × 400 g (14 oz) tin coconut milk
20 fresh mint leaves

PUY LENTIL TOPPING
200 g (7 oz/1 cup) cooked Lazy Lentils (page 36) or store-bought
1 tbsp extra-virgin olive oil
zest of ½ unwaxed lemon
sea salt and freshly ground black pepper

TO SERVE
toasted pumpkin seeds
fresh mint or purple shiso leaves
sea salt and freshly ground black pepper
extra-virgin olive oil
toasted sourdough garlic bread

To prepare the lentil topping, add the cooked lentils to a small bowl, stir through the oil and zest and seasoning to taste. Set aside.

For the soup, heat the oil in a large saucepan on a medium-low heat. Roughly chop the onion and garlic, add them to the pan along with the ginger and sauté for about 10 minutes or until the onion begins to soften. Add the peas and broccoli to and sauté for a further 5 minutes. Add the stock and season to taste. Bring to the boil, reduce the heat and simmer until the vegetables are tender, stirring occasionally so the soup doesn't burn. Remove from the heat and stir through the coconut milk and mint. Using an immersion (hand) blender or food processor, blend until smooth.

Top with a sprinkling of lentils, pumpkin seeds, mint and some seasoning and a drizzle of oil, along with toast on the side.

Shakshuka on a Bed of Hummus

Serves 4

Prep + cook time:
35 minutes

Cracking a few eggs straight into a pan of bubbling, spicy, cumin-flavoured tomato sauce is one of the easiest and most wonderful one-pot dinners that we know, especially when it's served with some bread on the side, for scooping up the sauce. However, ladling the shakshuka on top of a thin bed of hummus makes it even better. The rich and creamy hummus balances the sweet, spicy and tangy shakshuka just perfectly, and it also turns it into the ultimate comfort food.

Whether you serve this shakshuka with or without hummus, it is a very easy recipe to get creative with. The red (bell) pepper can be replaced with finely diced aubergine (eggplant) or courgette (zucchini). Spinach or kale can be added to the tomato sauce and a pinch of saffron can be added for extra flair.

2 tbsp extra-virgin olive oil
1 onion, peeled
3 cloves of garlic, peeled
½ fresh red chilli, seeded
1 red (bell) pepper, trimmed
½ tsp harissa, plus extra to serve
½ tsp ground cumin
⅓ quantity (720 ml/24 fl oz/3 cups)
    Big-batch Tomato Sauce* (page 22)
    or tinned tomatoes
sea salt and freshly ground black
    pepper
4 free-range eggs

TO SERVE
Heavenly Hummus (page 26)
    or store-bought hummus
roughly chopped fresh flat-leaf
    parsley or rocket (arugula) leaves
Za'atar (page 202) (optional)
sea salt and freshly ground black
    pepper
extra-virgin olive oil
warmed pita breads or gluten-free
    flatbreads

If you haven't got any tomato sauce to hand, simply add 2 × 400 g (14 oz) tins of chopped tomatoes and 3 tbsp of tomato purée (paste) instead and simmer for 30 minutes instead of 5 minutes. Make sure to taste and season appropriately.

TIP:
For a vegan alternative, replace the eggs with some fried tofu.

Heat the oil in a large frying pan (skillet) on a medium-low heat. Finely chop the onion, garlic and chilli and cut the red pepper into chunks. Transfer to the pan along with the harissa and cumin and sauté for about 15 minutes or until the onion has softened. Add the tomato sauce or tinned tomatoes and season to taste. Bring to the boil, then simmer until the sauce is heated through, stirring from time to time so the sauce doesn't burn. Add more water if the sauce becomes too dry.

Create four small wells in the sauce and crack an egg into each one. Cook the eggs to your liking. Spread out a layer of hummus in 4 bowls. Ladle one egg and shakshuka on top of the hummus. Top with extra harissa, a handful of parsley or rocket, some za'atar and seasoning. Serve with a drizzle of oil and some flatbread.

At the Weekend

'I'll finish this later. I am just going to go out and pick up some things in the supermarket', I hear him saying before the door shuts. It's 6.45 p.m. on a Saturday evening, we have guests arriving in 15 minutes and David seems to think now is a good time to start shopping for an extra recipe, instead of just finishing the one we agreed on. Welcome to our kitchen.

David is good at many things, but planning isn't one of them. He is always late, always changes his plans and always wants to add dishes to the table at the last minute. And still, he is never stressed, even though he is standing there with a half-finished dinner when the guests arrive.

'It's much nicer to be cooking together with the guests anyway,' is his response. I don't know, maybe he's right? Involving the guests in the dinner preparations is often more fun than having everything ready. Giving them a knife and a chopping board makes for more relaxed conversations than standing with a glass in hand. I just wish it was the original plan and not the constant last-minute excuse.

Regardless of whether you are preparing food before a gathering or together with your guests or family, these are all great meals for weekend get-togethers. They might take a little extra time to prepare but they are worth it. Most of them are main dishes but we have also included a Farinata with Roasted Grapes and Ricotta (page 153) which is a gorgeous little starter to serve with a glass of white wine, and the pumpkin smørrebrød (page 177) which we serve either on a brunch table or as a starter. There are a couple of hearty salads, a vegetarian take on bouillabaisse and beautifully roasted aubergine (eggplant) halves that all are quite impressive. But we've also included the more chilled Family-style Tortilla Bowls (page 179) and Cauli 'Fish' and Chips (page 157) which are both instant child favourites. *Luise*

Farinata with Roasted Grapes and Ricotta

Serves 2 (or 4 as a starter)

Prep + cook time:
35 minutes

Farinata is a simple Italian pancake bread (identical to the French socca). It's made from chickpea (gram) flour, water and oil and, when cooked right, it is crispy on the outside with a warm and soft centre. We love to serve it as a starter when we have friends over for dinner, and we've jazzed up the traditional version by topping it with roasted grapes and creamy ricotta. Keep it rustic and serve it hot straight from the pan, with a glass of wine on the side.

1 tbsp fresh rosemary leaves
150 g (5¼ oz/1 cup) chickpea
  (gram) flour
4 tbsp extra-virgin olive oil
1 tsp sea salt flakes
freshly ground black pepper

FOR THE ROASTED GRAPES
150 g (5¼ oz/1 cup) seedless red
  grapes, on the vine if possible

TO SERVE
rocket (arugula) leaves
250 g (8¾ oz/1 cup) ricotta
sea salt and freshly ground black
  pepper
extra-virgin olive oil
balsamic vinegar

To prepare the roasted grapes, start by lining a baking tray with parchment paper.

Leave half of the grapes on the vine and pull off the rest. Transfer them to the baking tray and place in the oven. Set the oven to 275°C (525°F/Gas mark 9) and bake for 30–35 minutes or until juicy, wrinkly and caramelised. Set aside.

Meanwhile, prepare the farinata. Finely chop the rosemary leaves and add them to a large mixing bowl along with the flour, 250 ml (8 fl oz) of lukewarm water, half the oil and all the salt. Season to taste with pepper, whisk until well combined and set aside to thicken for at least 20 minutes.

Heat a medium-sized ovenproof cast-iron frying pan (skillet) in the oven. Once hot, coat the base and sides of the pan with the rest of the oil. Whisk the batter, then pour it into the frying pan to create an even layer. Place under the grill (broiler) and grill for 10–15 minutes or until cooked and golden.

Remove from the grill and cut into triangles. Serve straight from the pan, topped with a handful of rocket, a dollop of ricotta, some roasted grapes, a sprinkling of seasoning and drizzle of oil and vinegar.

TIP:
For a vegan alternative, replace the ricotta with a vegan soft cheese.

Black Rice, Lentil and Aubergine Pilaf

Serves 6

Prep + cook time:
45 minutes

The taste, texture and visual aspects of this salad are all rather appealing. It's packed with spices, has lots of filling elements and an armada of shades and colours. Technically, I would put this recipe somewhere in between a pilaf and a salad, as it has both the qualities of flavoured rice and a generous, hearty salad.

200 g (7 oz/1 cup) black or brown rice,* rinsed
200 g (7 oz/1 cup) green lentils, rinsed
1 tsp cardamom seeds
1 tsp sea salt
8 tbsp extra-virgin olive oil
juice of 1½ lemons
½ tsp ground cumin
½ tsp ground turmeric
½ tsp chilli powder
a pinch of sea salt flakes
1 aubergine (eggplant), stem removed
½ cucumber, topped and tailed, halved and seeds removed

½ red onion, peeled
1 ripe avocado, stone removed and flesh scooped out
100 g (3½ oz/2 cups) spinach
1 handful (25 g/¾ oz) fresh mint, leaves picked
20 unsulphured dried apricot halves
sea salt and freshly ground black pepper

TO SERVE
full-fat plain unsweetened yoghurt
pistachio nuts, roughly chopped

Rice can differ in cooking time. Choose a variety with the same cooking time as your lentils.

TIPS:
If you are sensitive to raw onion, massage the slices with 1 tbsp of lemon juice to make the flavour less intense and easier to digest.

For a nut-free alternative, replace the pistachio nuts with pumpkin seeds or sunflower seeds.

Preheat the oven to 200°C (400°F/Gas mark 6) and line a baking tray with parchment paper.

Place the rice, lentils, cardamom, salt and 1 litre (32 fl oz/4 cups) water in a medium-sized saucepan, cover and bring to the boil, then simmer for about 30 minutes or until tender and the water has been absorbed. Drain any excess water and set aside to cool.

Meanwhile, place half the oil, juice of 1 lemon, spices and salt in a medium-sized mixing bowl and whisk until combined.

Cut the aubergine into bite-sized pieces, add to the bowl, toss until well coated and transfer to the baking tray. Bake for 25–30 minutes or until tender and golden. Set aside to cool.

In the meantime, slice the cucumber, finely slice the onion, cut the avocado into bite-sized pieces and roughly chop the spinach, mint and apricots.

Put the rice and lentils in a serving bowl, add the remaining oil and juice of ½ lemon and toss to coat. Add the aubergine and the rest of the ingredients, season to taste and gently toss to combine. Serve topped yoghurt and pistachio nuts.

Liberate
[Information Age]
In Germany, Deutsche Post has
used drones to deliver prescrip-
tion drugs. A Shanghai company
uses them to convey cakes.
Drones aren't just for deliver-
ing goods. Scientists have used

Cauli 'Fish' and Chips

Makes 20–24 / Serves 4

Prep + cook time:
1 hour 30 minutes

Our freezer has three drawers. The top one is reserved for frozen berries, fruit and ice cream. It's always jam-packed. The second drawer is for all kinds of frozen veggies, usually a mix of peas, spinach, broccoli and corn. In the third drawer we keep our leftovers. There are often a couple of unmarked and forgotten soups and curries in the bottom, a bag of bread, a roll of Perfect Pesto (page 25) and, on lucky days, we also have a bag of these veggie 'fish' bites. They are our vegetarian take on a classic. As with most food that you can eat with your hands, these are very kid-friendly, but adults seem to love them too.

Even if they don't imitate fish exactly, they do have the right light feeling and with a squeeze of lemon on top and dunked in tartare sauce it all feels rather convincing. We have created the recipe so that the potatoes are baked at the same time as the 'fish', which is also very convenient. Make a double batch of the cauli 'fish' so you've got an extra portion in the freezer for lucky days.

CAULI 'FISH'
2 tbsp virgin coconut oil
    or extra-virgin olive oil
1 onion, peeled
1 leek, washed, trimmed and tops
    removed
2 cloves of garlic, peeled
1 medium cauliflower (600 g/1 lb 5 oz)
    head and trimmed stalk
1 courgette (zucchini) (130 g/4½ oz)
2 free-range eggs
120 g (4¼ oz/1 scant cup) almond flour
150 g (5¼ oz/¾ cup) cottage cheese
zest of 1 large unwaxed lemon
½ tsp sea salt

POTATO CHIPS
500 g (1 lb) baby potatoes, scrubbed
2 tbsp extra-virgin olive oil
sea salt and freshly ground black
    pepper

TARTARE SAUCE
2 tbsp capers, drained
3 tbsp chopped fresh flat-leaf parsley
    leaves
250 ml (8 fl oz/1 cup) plain yoghurt
juice of 1 lemon
sea salt and freshly ground black
    pepper

TO SERVE
fresh flat-leaf parsley leaves
lemon wedges

continues overleaf

Preheat the oven to 200°C (400°F/Gas mark 6) and line 2 baking trays with parchment paper.

Heat the oil for the cauli 'fish' in a large frying pan (skillet) on a medium-low heat. Finely chop the onion, leek and garlic, transfer to the pan and sauté for about 15 minutes or until the onion and leek have softened. Remove from the heat and set aside.

Meanwhile, roughly chop the cauliflower, transfer to a food processor and blend until the texture resembles coarse breadcrumbs, then set aside. Grate the courgette, squeeze out the excess water (you should end up with about 130 g/ 4½ oz/1 cup of grated courgette) and set aside. Crack the eggs into a large mixing bowl and whisk until the yolks and whites are combined. Add the sautéed vegetables, cauliflower, courgette and the rest of the cauli 'fish' ingredients and mix until combined.

Dip 2 spoons (or your hands) into hot water and shake off the excess water. Take a generous scoop of the cauli 'fish' mixture and pass it repeatedly between the spoons, turning and smoothing each side until a neat quenelle or ball is formed. Place the quenelles on one of the baking trays.

To prepare the potato chips, quarter the potatoes, pat dry with kitchen paper and transfer to the second baking tray. Drizzle over the oil, season with salt and pepper and toss until well coated.

Bake the cauli 'fish' and potato chips at the same time for 25–30 minutes or until cooked, golden and crispy.

In the meantime, roughly chop the capers and transfer them to a small mixing bowl. Add the rest of the tartare sauce ingredients, season with salt and pepper and mix until combined.

Serve the cauli 'fish' accompanied by some chips and topped with a dollop of tartare sauce, scattering of parsley and squeeze of lemon juice.

Burrata, Peach and Grilled Vegetable Salad

Serves 4

Prep + cook time:
35 minutes

There is a café located on the opposite side of town from us that serves the most incredible salads – always full of flavour, colourful and pretty, like pieces of art. We rarely leave the southern parts of the city, where we live, but when we do it is often for their salad.

Lately, we have started recreating a similar version at home. The key elements are a creamy burrata, a mix of raw and grilled vegetables, peach slices, dots of beetroot (beet) spread and a drizzle of herb oil.

2 red (bell) peppers,
20 red cherry tomatoes, on the vine
2 tbsp extra-virgin olive oil
sea salt and freshly ground black
    pepper
2 ripe peaches, stones removed,
    or pears, cored
2 small, raw yellow beetroot (beet),
    trimmed, tops removed and peeled
2 handfuls (50 g/1¾ oz) rocket
    (arugula) leaves or mesclun
8 yellow (or red) cherry tomatoes,
    halved
20 Kalamata olives, drained and pitted
2 balls (250 g/8¾ oz) burrata or
    buffalo mozzarella, drained

HERB OIL
1 handful (25 g/¾ oz) fresh mint
1 handful (25 g/¾ oz) flat-leaf parsley
1 handful (25 g/¾ oz) fresh basil
6 tbsp extra-virgin olive oil
juice of ½ lemon
sea salt and freshly ground black
    pepper

TO SERVE
Beetroot Spread (page 211)
balsamic vinegar

Preheat the oven to 200°C (400°F/Gas mark 6) and line a baking tray with parchment paper.

Cut the peppers into 2 cm (¾ inch) thick slices and transfer to the baking tray along with the cherry tomatoes. Drizzle over the oil, season to taste and toss until well coated. Bake for 20–25 minutes or until tender and slightly charred.

Meanwhile, prepare the herb oil. Place all of the herb oil ingredients in a food processor, season to taste, pulse until coarsely mixed and set aside.

To assemble the salad, cut the peaches into wedges, shave the beetroot and arrange on top of the rocket, with the peppers, baked and fresh tomatoes and olives. Break the burrata into large pieces and place on top. Serve with dollops of beetroot spread and a drizzle of herb oil and vinegar.

TIP:
Burrata is an exclusive form of mozzarella that is formed into a pouch and filled with soft, stringy curd and cream that oozes out when torn. Since it's quite expensive, this is a typical party salad perfect for impressing friends with. Buffalo mozzarella can be used instead, if you wish.

Double-sweater Minestrone with Rice

Serves 6

Prep + cook time:
1 hour

Rich, hearty and full of flavour, this very Italian soup is what we turn to during those harsh Scandinavian winter days when we need to wear double sweaters and triple socks to stay warm.

It's common to find pasta in minestrone but we much prefer rice. It feels like a more adult option and it has a nicer textural bite. Since none of us find any joy in washing the dishes, we also enjoy the fact that the rice is cooked in the soup and not in a separate pot. The addition of beans makes it substantial and filling enough for a dinner.

2 tbsp extra-virgin olive oil
1 onion, peeled
2 celery stalks, trimmed
4 cloves of garlic, peeled
2 carrots, tops removed and peeled
1 handful (25 g/¾ oz) fresh Italian
    herbs, leaves picked (e.g. basil,
    flat-leaf parsley, thyme, oregano)
¼ tsp chilli flakes
¼ tsp smoked paprika
2 tbsp tomato purée (paste)
2 × 400 g (14 oz) tins chopped
    tomatoes
1.5 litres (6 cups) vegetable stock
100 g (3½ oz/½ cup) wholegrain
    rice, rinsed

sea salt and freshly ground black
    pepper
1 × 400 g (14 oz) tin mixed beans,
    drained and rinsed
1 handful (25 g/¾ oz) fresh basil and
    flat-leaf parsley, leaves picked

TO SERVE
freshly grated pecorino or Parmesan
torn fresh basil leaves
sea salt and freshly ground black
    pepper
extra-virgin olive oil

TIPS:
Many hard cheeses (like pecorino and Parmesan) contain animal rennet, which technically isn't a vegetarian product, but there are rennet-free options available: they are often marked as vegetarian-friendly (or kosher cheese) but just ask in a cheese department if you are unsure.

For a nut-free alternative, replace the pine nuts with pumpkin seeds or sunflower seeds.

For a vegan alternative, simply skip the pecorino. It is rich and tasty nonetheless.

Heat the oil in a large saucepan on a medium-low heat. Finely chop the onion, celery and garlic and roughly chop the carrots and herbs. Add the vegetables, herbs and spices to the pan and sauté for about 15 minutes or until the onion has softened. Add the tomato purée, tinned tomatoes, stock and rice and season to taste. Bring to the boil, reduce the heat and simmer for 30–45 minutes or until the rice is cooked, stirring from time to time so the soup doesn't burn on the base of the pan. Remove from the heat and stir through the beans and herbs.

Serve topped with a sprinkling of pecorino or Parmesan, basil, seasoning and a drizzle of oil.

Beetroot and Goat's Cheese Quiche

Serves 4

Prep + cook time:
1 hour and 10 minutes
+ 30 minutes for the
pastry to rest

Now might be a good time to ask: do you like beetroot (beet)? We've heard that some people loathe it but we obviously don't feel the same way. This sweet, earthy colour-explosion of a root is incredibly versatile and lovely to use in cooking. In this book, it features in bread, juice, crêpes, burgers and salads.

Here, it is the star ingredient of a quiche, paired with its two best friends, goat's (chèvre) cheese and walnuts. Tons of mint add a sharp contrast to the beetroot's sweetness and nuttiness. If the beetroot has healthy-looking greens, we use them in this recipe, too. Otherwise they can be replaced with spinach, chard or kale.

If you answered 'no' to the question above, may we just apologise for our obsession with the root (but deep inside we still hope that you will give our beetroot recipes a chance and that they will help you overcome your aversion).

PASTRY
100 g (3½ oz/1 cup) rolled oats
50 g (1¾ oz/½ cup) almond or
    walnut flour
50 g (1¾ oz /⅓ cup) rice or spelt flour
40 g (1½ oz/¼ cup) linseeds
2 tbsp arrowroot (or potato starch)
½ tsp sea salt
80 g (3 oz) butter, cubed and chilled,
    or virgin coconut oil, plus extra
    to grease

FILLING
250 g (8¾ oz) raw beetroot (beet),
    trimmed and peeled, tops reserved
    for filling
1 tbsp virgin coconut oil
1 red onion, peeled
3 cloves of garlic, peeled
2 tsp fresh thyme leaves
    or 1 tsp dried thyme

FILLING (cont.)
20 fresh mint leaves
100 g (3½ oz/2 cups) raw beetroot
    (beet) tops or spinach
2 tbsp organic apple cider vinegar
    or lemon juice
2 tbsp runny honey, plus extra
    to drizzle
sea salt and freshly ground black
    pepper
3 free-range eggs
120 ml (4 fl oz/½ cup) plant-based
    milk of choice
100 g (3½ oz) soft goat's (chèvre)
    cheese
12 walnuts

TO SERVE
full-fat plain Turkish or Greek yoghurt
    (optional)
fresh mint leaves

TIP:
For a nut-free alternative, replace the almond or walnut flour with pumpkin seed, sunflower seed or linseed flour.

continues overleaf

Place all of the dry pastry ingredients in a food processor and blend until the texture resembles coarse flour. Add the butter and blend until combined, then add 4 tablespoons of ice-cold water, a tablespoon at a time, and pulse until the mixture comes together. Remove the dough from the processor, knead it slightly then shape it into a ball. Wrap in cling film (plastic wrap) and set aside in the fridge to rest for at least 30 minutes.

Preheat the oven to 180°C (350°F/Gas mark 4) and grease a 20 cm (8 inch) diameter quiche dish or tart tin.

Unwrap the chilled dough. Place it in the dish or tin and press it out evenly to cover the base and sides, making sure that it's flush with the edges of the dish. Prick the pastry base with a fork and bake blind for about 12 minutes or until the pastry is firm and slightly golden. Remove from the oven, set aside and reduce the oven temperature to 170°C (340°F/Gas mark 3½).

Grate the beetroot on the fine or medium side of a box grater then set aside. Heat the oil in the pan on a medium-low heat. Thinly slice the onion, finely chop the garlic and add them to the pan, along with the thyme. Sauté for about 15 minutes or until the onion has softened and remove from the heat.

Roughly chop the mint, add to the pan along with the beetroot tops or spinach, vinegar or lemon juice and honey and stir through while the vegetables are still warm so that the greens wilt. Season to taste with salt and pepper and set aside.

Crack the eggs into a medium-sized mixing bowl, add the milk and whisk until combined. Add the vegetables to the bowl and stir until combined.

Spread the grated beetroot over the pastry base, pour the quiche filling on top, leaving the outer edge uncovered so that the beetroot is still visible, and crumble over the goat's cheese.

Roughly chop the walnuts, scatter on top, drizzle with honey and bake for 30–45 minutes or until the filling is firm and golden. Remove from the oven and set aside to cool slightly before slicing.

Serve the quiche slightly warm, topped with a dollop of yoghurt, if desired, a few mint leaves and a drizzle of honey.

Baked Portobello Mushrooms in White Wine and Vegetables

Serves 4

Prep + cook time:
1 hour and 10 minutes

Three things come to mind when I think about this recipe. First, the smell of white wine, lemon, olive oil, garlic, capers and thyme that hits me when I open the oven door. So fragrant and intense. Second, the texture of the vegetables that cook in the sauce; soft and tender that they almost melt on your tongue. Finally, those portobello mushrooms. They become really juicy and delicious and add a pleasant meatiness to each plate.

We top the dish with feta and pistachios before baking, which makes it rich, tangy and crunchy and serve it on top of polenta, rice or lentils. *David*

1 onion, peeled

1 fennel bulb, trimmed

2 carrots, tops removed and peeled

20 cherry tomatoes

4 cloves of garlic, peeled and bruised

2 tbsp capers, drained

120 ml (4 fl oz/½ cup) white wine

juice of ½ lemon

3 tbsp extra-virgin olive oil

6 sprigs fresh thyme, leaves picked

sea salt and freshly ground black pepper

4 portobello mushrooms, cleaned and trimmed

100 g (3½ oz) feta

1 handful (25 g/¾ oz) fresh basil

35 g (1¼ oz/¼ cup) pistachio nuts

TO SERVE

soft-cooked polenta, rice or black lentils (enough for 4 servings)

Preheat the oven to 200°C (400°F/Gas mark 6).

Coarsely chop the onion, fennel, carrots and tomatoes (into roughly 1–2 cm/ ½–¾ inch pieces) and place them in a 30 × 20 cm (12 × 8 inch) ovenproof baking dish along with the whole garlic cloves and capers. Add the wine, 120 ml (4 fl oz/ ½ cup) water, lemon juice, oil and 4 sprigs thyme and season generously. Toss to combine, place in the oven and bake for 25 minutes.

Remove from the oven, make 4 gaps among the vegetables in the dish and place the mushrooms in them, cap side down. Crumble over the feta, and roughly chop the basil, remaining thyme leaves and pistachios and scatter them over the dish.

Bake for 20–30 minutes more or until the vegetables are tender, basting the tops of the mushrooms from time to time to prevent them from drying out. Remove from the oven and ladle on top of a base of polenta, rice or black lentils.

TIPS:
For a nut-free alternative, replace the pistachio nuts with pumpkin seeds or sunflower seeds.

For a vegan alternative, sprinkle over breadcrumbs instead of feta.

Popeye Polpette (Spinach, Quinoa and Ricotta 'Meatballs')

Makes about 24 polpette
Serves 6

Prep + cook time:
40 minutes

Would you believe me if I said that my middle name is Popeye? It actually is. I had such wide shoulders when I was born that my parents thought that giving me the name of the spinach-loving sailor, was fitting. Little did they realise how that name would grow to suit me as I became a vegetable advocate and spinach lover (still not entirely there with the tattoo and biceps though).

These polpette are airy and light, yet comfortably nourishing. We often steal a few polpette straight from the baking tray, but they are even better served tangled in linguine or courgette (zucchini) noodles with tomato sauce poured over. Our Big-batch Tomato Sauce (page 22) is perfect for this. *David*

100 g (3½ oz/⅔ cup) sunflower seeds, toasted
300 g (10½ oz/2 cups) cooked quinoa (Quick Quinoa page 31)
250 g (8¾ oz) fresh ricotta
100 g (3½ oz/2 cups) baby spinach or regular spinach, stems removed
1 handful (25 g/¾ oz) fresh basil
1 tbsp extra-virgin olive oil
zest and juice of ½ unwaxed lemon
sea salt and freshly ground black pepper

TO SERVE
courgette (zucchini) noodles or cooked pasta of choice
⅓ quantity (720 ml/24 fl oz/3 cups) Big-batch Tomato Sauce (page 22)
freshly grated pecorino or Parmesan
pine nuts, toasted
torn fresh basil leaves
sea salt and freshly ground black pepper
extra-virgin olive oil

Preheat the oven to 200°C (400°F/Gas mark 6) and line a baking tray with parchment paper.

Place the sunflower seeds in a food processor and blend until the texture resembles coarse flour. Add the rest of the polpette ingredients, season to taste and blend until smooth. Dip two spoons (or your hands) into hot water and shake off the excess water. Take a generous scoop of the polpette mix, and pass the mixture repeatedly between the spoons, turning and smoothing each side until a neat quenelle or ball is formed. Transfer to the baking tray and repeat with the rest of the mixture. Bake for about 20 minutes or until cooked and golden with a crispy outside.

Serve on top of courgette noodles or pasta with tomato sauce. Top with cheese, pine nuts, basil, seasoning and a drizzle of oil.

TIP:
For a nut-free alternative, replace the pine nuts with pumpkin seeds or sunflower seeds.

Chermoula Baked Aubergine with Spiced Chickpeas

Serves 4

Prep + cook time:
1 hour

When aubergine (eggplant) is baked until almost charred and tender inside, it's a real gem of a vegetable. Here, we halve the aubergines, score the flesh and rub them with a spicy chermoula marinade, then bake them until tender with spicy chickpeas (garbanzo beans) and red onion slices, and top with a citrus salad of orange and parsley. It's a flavour explosion, fun to eat and much easier to prepare than it appears, since the oven does most of the work. Make sure not to under-bake the aubergine, though, as it will be bitter and have stringy flesh.

4 aubergines (eggplants)

CHERMOULA
4 cloves of garlic, peeled
4 tsp ground cumin
4 tsp ground coriander
2 tsp smoked paprika
½ tsp sea salt
½–1 tsp chilli flakes
6 tbsp extra-virgin olive oil
juice of 1 lemon

SPICED CHICKPEAS
3 red onions, peeled
1 × 400 g (14 oz) tin chickpeas
    (garbanzo beans),* drained
    and rinsed
½ tsp ground cinnamon
¼ tsp ground ginger
¼–½ tsp chilli flakes
2 tbsp extra-virgin olive oil
juice of ½ lemon
sea salt and freshly ground black
    pepper

CITRUS SALAD
2 oranges, peeled
35 g (1¼ oz/¼ cup) almonds, toasted
1 handful (25 g/¾ oz) flat-leaf parsley,
    leaves picked
1 handful (25 g/¾ oz) rocket (arugula)
    leaves
4 tbsp sultanas or raisins
1 tbsp extra-virgin olive oil
sea salt and freshly ground black
    pepper

TO SERVE
full-fat plain unsweetened yoghurt
warmed flatbreads or gluten-free
    flatbreads

200 g (7 oz/1½ cups) cooked chickpeas (garbanzo beans) (page 26).

TIPS:
For a nut-free alternative, replace the almonds with pumpkin seeds.

For a vegan alternative, replace the yoghurt with a plant-based yoghurt such as coconut, soy or oat.

continues overleaf

Preheat the oven to 200°C (400°F/Gas mark 6) and line 2 baking trays with parchment paper.

Cut the aubergines in half lengthwise, score the flesh in a crisscross pattern and transfer to one of the baking trays. Finely chop the garlic and transfer to a small mixing bowl along with the rest of the chermoula ingredients. Mix until combined then rub over the scored aubergine flesh. Bake the aubergines for about 45 minutes or until tender, very soft and golden.

Meanwhile, prepare the spiced chickpeas. Cut the onions in half then 1 cm (½ inch) thick slices. Transfer to a medium-sized mixing bowl along with the rest of the spiced chickpeas ingredients. Season to taste with salt and pepper and toss until well coated in the oil and spices. Transfer to the second baking tray and bake for about 15 minutes or until the onions are tender and the chickpeas are slightly crunchy and golden.

In the meantime, prepare the citrus salad. Segment and roughly chop the oranges, roughly chop the almonds and parsley and tear the rocket. Transfer to a medium-sized mixing bowl along with the sultanas and oil. Season to taste with salt and pepper and mix until combined.

Serve the aubergine topped with some spiced chickpeas, a scattering of the citrus salad and a dollop of yoghurt, along with flatbreads on the side.

Roast Butternut and Rocket Smørrebrød

Serves 2

Prep + cook time:
10 minutes

While many countries have a culture of warm lunches, we Danes usually settle for an open-faced sandwich around noon. Smørrebrød isn't just a meal to us, it's a huge part of our food culture. In fact, the Danish words for 'sandwich' and 'food' are identical; only a preposition tells them apart.

The sandwich base is most commonly sourdough rye bread and, even though there is a wide range of popular toppings, I often try new combinations. Using roasted butternut is definitely out of the ordinary, but it has become a favourite of mine. It is smooth and sweet and works great on top of toasted rye. Thin slices of cucumber, lemon, rocket (aruglua) and chickpeas (garbanzo beans) add a pleasant contrast in flavour, colour and texture and chilli flakes add a little punch.

This is an ideal quick meal if you happen to have some Pumpkin Purée (page 28) in the fridge, and can also be beautiful on a brunch table. *Luise*

4 slices sourdough rye bread
½ small red onion, peeled
1 × 400 g (14 oz) tin chickpeas, (garbanzo beans)* drained and rinsed
250 g (8¾ oz/1 cup) Pumpkin Purée (page 28)
juice of ½ lemon
1 tbsp extra-virgin olive oil
¼ tsp chilli flakes

sea salt and freshly ground black pepper
½ cucumber, topped and tailed (organic if possible)

TO SERVE
rocket (arugula) leaves
sea salt flakes and freshly ground pepper (black or white)
extra-virgin olive oil

* Or 150 g (5¼ oz/1 cup) cooked chickpeas (garbanzo beans) (page 26).

TIPS:
For a gluten-free alternative, replace the sourdough rye bread with a gluten-free bread.

If you are sensitive to raw onion, massage the slices with 1 tbsp of lemon juice to make it less intense in flavour and easier to digest.

Toast the bread and finely slice the red onion.

Place the chickpeas in a medium-sized bowl and mash them with a fork. Add the purée, 1 tablespoon of the lemon juice, oil and chilli flakes, season to taste with salt and pepper and mix until combined.

To assemble, spoon the butternut mash onto the toast, thinly slice the cucumber and arrange on top of the mash, along with the onion. Serve topped with a handful of rocket, a sprinkling of salt and pepper, the remaining lemon juice and a drizzle of oil.

Family-style Tortilla Bowls

Serves 4

Prep + cook time:
30 minutes

This is a common scene on a Friday evening in our home: both kids hanging over the table, dipping warm tortilla chips (and fingers and sleeves) in various bowls. For Luise and I, this recipe is all about building our own Mexican-inspired tortilla bowl, but for the kids it's just another reason to eat with their hands.

We usually keep the ingredients in the bowls on the table quite simple and fresh; a mashed avocado bowl, herb bowl, bean bowl, greens and yoghurt. And we have a couple of favourites that we spend a little extra time on – a smoky tomato and walnut sauce, a herby mango and corn salsa and sweet and spicy cashew nuts. *David*

TOMATO AND WALNUT SAUCE
1 tbsp virgin coconut oil or olive oil
1 tsp ground cumin
1 tsp ground smoked paprika
1 tsp ground coriander
½ tsp chilli flakes (optional)
1 red (bell) pepper, seeds removed and finely chopped
⅓ quantity (720 ml/24 fl oz/3 cups) Big-batch Tomato Sauce (page 22) or tinned tomatoes*
150 g (5¼ oz/1½ cups) walnuts, coarsely chopped

MANGO AND CORN SALSA
1 ripe mango
1 fresh corn cob
½ fresh red chilli, seeded
1 large handful (30 g/1 oz) fresh coriander (cilantro), leaves picked
1 tbsp extra-virgin olive oil
juice of 1 lime, to taste
sea salt, to taste

SWEET AND SPICY CASHEW NUTS
2 tsp virgin coconut oil
½ tsp ground cayenne pepper
½ tsp ground cumin
1 tsp sea salt
125 g (4½ oz/1 cup) cashew nuts
1 tbsp pure maple syrup

TO SERVE
1 large bag of organic, GMO-free tortilla chips
2 ripe avocados, stones removed, flesh scooped out
1 red (bell) pepper, stalk, core and seeds removed
2 limes
1 × 400 g (14 oz) tin black beans or kidney beans, drained and rinsed thoroughly
250 ml (8¾ fl oz/1 cup) plain thick yoghurt
paprika, for sprinkling
1 bag mixed leafy green lettuce
fresh coriander (cilantro)

If you haven't got any tomato sauce prepared, simply add 2 × 400 g (14 oz) tins of chopped tomatoes and 3 tbsp tomato purée (paste) instead and cook for longer, as per the recipe. Make sure to taste and season appropriately.

continues overleaf

To make the tomato and walnut sauce, heat the oil in a saucepan and add the cumin, paprika, coriander and chilli (if using). Fry, stirring, until the spices are fragrant, then add the red pepper and cook for a couple of minutes. Add the tomato sauce or tinned tomatoes and cook for a further 5 minutes (20 minutes if using tinned), then stir in the walnuts. Remove from the heat and set aside.

For the mango and corn salsa, cut the mango in two halves along the stone. Scoop out and dice the flesh. Cut the corn kernels off the cob, finely chop the chilli and roughly chop the coriander. Place all of the ingredients in a bowl and drizzle over the olive oil and lime juice. Season with salt and toss to combine.

For the sweet and spicy cashew nuts, heat the coconut oil and spices in a frying pan (skillet) on a medium-high heat. When fragrant, add the nuts and let them toast for a couple of minutes, stirring frequently. Drizzle over the maple syrup, stir and toast for a further 30 seconds, then remove from the heat and set aside.

Preheat the oven to 200°C (400°F/Gas mark 6). Scatter tortilla chips on a baking tray and bake for 5 minutes until warm and slightly toasted. Check on them often to make sure they do not burn.

Mash the avocado, dice the red pepper, and cut the limes into wedges. Place all the serving elements in bowls on the dinner table (as pictured on page 178) and let everyone build their own tortilla bowl.

Lemon Ricotta Lasagne for a Crowd

Serves 12

Prep + cook time:
1 hour 30 minutes

This is our version of a classic tomato lasagne – less stodgy but equally rich and heavy on the vegetables, with slices of portobello mushroom, roasted aubergine (eggplant) and kale layered between the pasta sheets, and halved cherry tomatoes covering the top. Instead of the traditional béchamel sauce, we use a tangy, fresh and rich lemon ricotta and it makes all the difference. Those tangy tones paired with the rich pasta and tomato sauce are a match made in heaven.

Since this is a rather time-consuming recipe, we have made sure that it feeds a crowd. We layer it in a large dish and it piles up really high. Any leftovers can be cut into single servings and frozen.

ROASTED AUBERGINE SLICES
3 aubergines (eggplants), stems removed
extra-virgin olive oil, to brush
sea salt

LEMON RICOTTA
750 g (1 lb 10 oz/3 cups) ricotta
1 large handful (30 g/1 oz) fresh basil, leaves roughly chopped
zest and juice of 2 unwaxed lemons
sea salt and freshly ground black pepper

TOMATO SAUCE
1.5 litres (6 cups) Big-batch Tomato Sauce (page 22)

TO ASSEMBLE
100 g (3½ oz/2 cups) spinach or curly kale, stems removed
2 portobello mushrooms, cleaned
500 g (17 oz) wholemeal or gluten-free lasagne sheets
500 g (1 lb/4 cups) cherry tomatoes
50 g (1¾ oz/½ cup) Parmesan or pecorino, grated

TO SERVE
1 large handful (30 g/1 oz) fresh basil, leaves roughly chopped

Preheat the oven to 200°C (400°F/Gas mark 6) and line 3 baking trays with parchment paper.

Cut the aubergines lengthwise into 5 mm (⅛ inch) slices, transfer to the baking trays, brush both sides of each slice with oil and season with salt. Bake for 20–30 minutes or until tender and golden. Set aside to cool.

To make the lemon ricotta, place all the ingredients in a large mixing bowl, season to taste, mix to combine and set aside. Chop the spinach and cut the mushrooms into 6 mm (¼ inch) thick slices.

TIP:
For an entirely grain-free version, you can use thinly shaved celery root instead of lasagne sheets.

To assemble, spread a cup of the tomato sauce over the base of a 35 × 25 × 7 cm (14 × 10 × 2¾ inch) ovenproof dish. Top with a layer of lasagne sheets, followed by a third of the lemon ricotta and aubergine slices. Repeat to form the second layer, adding half the mushrooms and spinach after the aubergine. Repeat to form the third layer, adding 2 cups of tomato sauce this time, and the rest of the mushrooms and spinach after the aubergine. To finish, spread 2 cups of the tomato sauce over the spinach. Halve the cherry tomatoes and arrange them cut side up on top of the tomato sauce. Sprinkle over the cheese and bake for 40–45 minutes or until the pasta is cooked and the top is golden. Serve topped with a scattering of basil and more grated cheese.

Middle-Eastern Cauliflower and Lentil Salad

Serves 4

Prep + cook time:
40 minutes

If you ask us which recipe in this book you should start with for a delicious dinner tonight, we would probably say this one. It has interesting flavours – sweet, warm and spicy – and is nourishing but not heavy, and impressive without being weird or complicated.

We have made this salad on countless occasions and it always seems right. It doesn't matter if it's a regular Tuesday or a family birthday dinner, everyone seems to enjoy the fragrant cauliflower, tahini-dressed lentils, toasted almonds, sweet dates and greens.

1 cauliflower, head and stalk
4 tbsp extra-virgin olive oil
½ tsp ground cumin
½ tsp ground cinnamon
½ tsp ground ginger
a pinch of ground cayenne pepper
sea salt and freshly ground black
    pepper
1 small red onion, peeled
400 g (14 oz/2 cups) cooked Lazy
    Lentils (page 36) or store-bought
12 soft or dried dates, pitted
75 g (2¾ oz/½ cup) almonds, toasted
100 g (3½ oz/2 cups) mâche or
    baby spinach

CREAMY TAHINI DRESSING
2 tbsp tahini
2 tbsp lemon juice
2 tbsp filtered water
2 tsp runny honey
sea salt and freshly ground black
    pepper

TIPS:
If you are sensitive to raw onion, massage the slices with 1 tbsp of lemon juice to make it easier to digest and less intense in flavour.

For a nut-free alternative, replace the almonds with pumpkin seeds or sunflower seeds.

Preheat the oven to 225°C (435°F/Gas mark 7) and line a baking tray with parchment paper. Cut the cauliflower into small florets and trim and roughly chop the stalk. Place in a mixing bowl, drizzle the oil and sprinkle the spices over the cauliflower, season and toss until well coated. Spread them on the tray and bake for 20–25 minutes, or until the cauliflower is tender and golden. Remove from the oven and set aside to cool.

Finely slice the red onion. Place all of the dressing ingredients in a serving bowl, season to taste and whisk to combine. Toss in the cooked lentils until well coated. Thinly slice the dates on the diagonal and roughly chop the almonds. Add half to the bowl along with the cauliflower, onion and spinach and combine. Scatter over of the remaining dates and almonds.

Vegan Mushroom and Lentil Burgers

Makes 10 burgers

Prep + cook time:
1 hour + 15 minutes

This is a proper vegan burger with a meaty texture and rich and earthy taste. Unlike the frozen versions you can find in supermarkets, this has no additives or weird ingredients. We simply make our burgers from a mix of mushrooms and lentils and sneak in some kale, capers and pumpkin seeds. Don't be intimidated if the burgers seem a little difficult to shape at first; once they are fried, they hold together really well.

In contrast to the traditional ketchup accompaniment, we use a rather untraditional chutney, which adds interesting flavours and sweetness to the burger. If you have time to make it, it will be worth your while.

These burgers can also be shaped into falafel-sized balls and baked in the oven.

SWEET POTATO FRIES
2 large sweet potatoes, scrubbed
3 tbsp extra-virgin olive oil
sea salt and freshly ground black
    pepper

LENTIL PATTIES
150 g (5¼ oz/1 cup) pumpkin seeds
4 tbsp extra-virgin olive oil
1 onion, peeled
½ handful (12 g/⅓ oz) cavolo nero
    or curly kale, stems removed
2 cloves of garlic, peeled
250 g (8¾ oz) mushrooms of choice,
    cleaned
400 g (14 oz/2 cups) Lazy Lentils
    (page 36) or store-bought
    cooked lentils

LENTIL PATTIES (cont.)
4 tbsp capers, drained and rinsed
2 tbsp tomato purée (paste)
½ tsp smoked paprika
sea salt and freshly ground black
    pepper
extra-virgin olive oil, virgin coconut
    oil, butter or ghee, to fry

TO SERVE
burger buns of choice
vegan mayonnaise
lettuce leaves
sprouts
sliced tomatoes
Apricot and Tomato Chutney
    (page 198)
sliced ripe avocado
drained gherkins

continues overleaf

To prepare the patties, place the pumpkin seeds in a food processor and blend until the texture resembles breadcrumbs. Heat half the oil in a large frying pan (skillet) on a medium-low heat. Roughly chop the onion, kale and garlic, transfer to the pan and sauté for about 10 minutes or until the onion has softened, then transfer to the food processor.

Heat the rest of the oil in the pan on a medium-high heat. Roughly chop the mushrooms, transfer to the pan and sauté (without stirring) for about 5 minutes or until golden. Turn them over and sauté for a further 5 minutes or until tender and golden before transferring to the food processor. Add the rest of the patty ingredients (except for the frying oil) to the food processor, season to taste with salt and pepper and pulse until combined but still coarse. Transfer one quarter of the mixture to a large mixing bowl and blend the rest of the mixture until smooth. Transfer the rest of the mixture to the bowl and mix until combined.

Use your hands to shape the mixture into 10 patties. Heat 1 tablespoon of oil in a large non-stick frying pan or griddle pan on a medium-high heat. Once hot, fry the patties in batches for a few minutes or until the base is golden. Carefully flip each patty with a spatula and fry the other side for a further few minutes or until golden.*

To make the fries, preheat the oven to 200°C (400°F/Gas mark 6) and line 2 baking trays with parchment paper. Cut the sweet potatoes into thin chips, transfer to the trays, drizzle over the oil, season to taste with salt and pepper and toss until well coated. Spread them out on the trays (make sure that they don't touch, for the crispiest result). Bake for about 20 minutes, then turn up the heat to max and bake for a few more minutes to crisp them even further. They are done when the edges are just slightly burnt.

Serve the patties inside buns spread with mayonnaise and filled with lettuce, sprouts, tomato, chutney and avocado and accompanied by sliced gherkins and some fries.

Alternatively, bake the burgers in the oven on a lined baking tray at 200°C (400°F/Gas mark 6) for 20 minutes, flip and bake for a further 5–10 minutes or until golden on both sides.

Millet and Butternut Winter Salad

Serves 4

Prep + cook time:
45 minutes

We love adding millet to our salads to make them more nourishing. Millet might not be as common as rice, couscous or quinoa, but it has been an important food staple for the past 10,000 years. A gluten-free, easy-to-digest seed, millet is high in important minerals, iron and B vitamins and has a soft, grain-like texture when cooked. It is similar to couscous but slightly creamier, with a light, nutty flavour.

1 broccoli or Romanesco, head and
   trimmed stalk
½ butternut squash, peeled and
   seeds removed
2 tbsp extra-virgin olive oil
sea salt and freshly ground black
   pepper
120 g (4¼ oz/½ cup) hulled uncooked
   millet, rinsed
¼ raw celeriac, trimmed and peeled
2 tbsp lemon juice
100 g (3½ oz/2 cups) kale, stems
   removed

CREAMY DIJON DRESSING
2 tbsp Dijon mustard
2 tbsp extra-virgin olive oil
2 tbsp lemon juice
1 tbsp runny honey
sea salt and freshly ground black
   pepper

TO SERVE
halved seedless red grapes
roughly chopped toasted hazelnuts

Preheat the oven to 180°C (350°F/Gas mark 4) and line a baking tray with parchment paper. Cut the broccoli head into small florets and set aside. Cut the broccoli stalk and butternut squash into bite-sized pieces and transfer to the baking tray. Drizzle over the oil, season with salt and pepper and toss until well coated. Bake for 10 minutes, then add the florets and bake for a further 20 minutes or until the vegetables are tender and golden.

Meanwhile, place the millet and 250 ml (8 fl oz/1 cup) water in a saucepan, cover and bring to the boil, then simmer for about 10 minutes or until the millet is tender and has absorbed all of the water. Remove from the heat and set aside.

Cut the celeriac into matchsticks, transfer to a small bowl, massage with the lemon juice and set aside. Place all of the dressing ingredients, plus 2 tablespoons of water, in a large bowl, season to taste and whisk to combine.

Add the kale to the serving bowl and gently massage it until it is well coated in the dressing. Add the baked vegetables, millet and celeriac and toss until combined. Serve topped with a scattering of grapes and hazelnuts.

TIPS:
Brussels sprouts can be roasted instead of broccoli, pomegranate seeds can replace the grapes and sweet potatoes can be used instead of pumpkin.

For a nut-free alternative, replace the hazelnuts with pumpkin seeds or sunflower seeds.

Vegetarian Bouillabaisse

When I was growing up, the scent of saffron in the kitchen meant two things: 1) We are having guests for dinner tomorrow. 2) My dad is cooking. You see, bouillabaisse Provençale was the only dish he knew how to cook. In his defence, he did master it. He made it a day ahead, to let the flavours develop even further.

Our version is heavy on vegetables, with potatoes instead of the fish and baked fennel slices on top to imitate crayfish. Like him, we serve it with aïoli. *David*

500 ml (16 fl oz/2 cups) vegetable
   stock
1 tsp saffron threads or
   ½ tsp saffron powder
4 tbsp extra-virgin olive oil
2 onions, peeled
4 cloves of garlic, peeled
2 tsp fennel seeds
1 tsp aniseeds
3 carrots, tops removed and peeled
2 parsnips, tops removed and peeled
2 low-starch potatoes, peeled
1 fennel bulb, stalks removed
250 ml (8 fl oz/1 cup) dry white wine
2 × 400 g (14 oz) tins chopped
   tomatoes
1 raw nori sheet, crushed
6 sprigs fresh thyme, leaves picked
sea salt and freshly ground black
   pepper
1 × 400 g (14 oz) tin white beans,
   drained and rinsed

BAKED FENNEL
1 fennel bulb, stalks removed, fronds
   set aside for garnish
extra-virgin olive oil, to brush
sea salt and freshly ground black
   pepper

FOR THE AÏOLI
2 cloves of garlic, peeled
2 free-range egg yolks*
1 tbsp lemon juice
120 ml (4 fl oz/½ cup) extra-virgin
   olive oil
120 ml (4 fl oz/½ cup) cold-pressed
   rapeseed oil
sea salt and freshly ground black
   pepper

TO SERVE
fresh thyme leaves
roughly chopped fresh fennel fronds
   and/or fresh dill
orange zest
sea salt and freshly ground black
   pepper
toasted sourdough bread or gluten-
   free bread rubbed with garlic

Raw egg is not recommended for infants, the elderly, pregnant women or people with weakened immune systems. Be sure to use pasteurised egg yolk instead.

TIP:
For a vegan alternative, replace the aïoli with a vegan aïoli.

continues overleaf

Preheat the oven to 225°C (435°F/Gas mark 7) and line a baking tray with parchment paper.

Bring the stock to the boil in a small saucepan, remove from the heat, add the saffron and set aside to steep while you prepare the bouillabaisse.

Heat the oil in a large saucepan on a medium-low heat. Roughly chop one onion, and finely chop the other, along with the garlic. Add the onions, garlic and spices to the pan and sauté for about 10 minutes or until the onions begin to soften. Cut the carrots and parsnips in half lengthwise and then into thick slices, and roughly chop the potatoes and fennel. Add the vegetables to the pan and sauté for a further 5 minutes, then add the wine. Once the alcohol has evaporated, add the stock and saffron, tomatoes, nori and thyme, and season to taste with salt and pepper. Bring to the boil, reduce the heat and simmer for 45–60 minutes or until the vegetables are tender, stirring from time to time so the bouillabaisse doesn't burn on the base of the pan. You may need to add more stock or water to loosen the sauce if it becomes too dry.

Meanwhile, prepare the baked fennel. Cut the remaining fennel lengthwise into 1.5 cm (⅝ inch) thick slices, brush with oil, season to taste with salt and pepper and transfer to the baking tray. Bake for 20–30 minutes or until the fennel is tender and caramelised. Remove from the oven and set aside.

To prepare the aïoli, finely chop the garlic and set aside. Place the egg yolks and lemon juice in a small mixing bowl and whisk together until combined. Whisking continuously, slowly drizzle in the oils. Once the sauce has thickened, season to taste with salt and pepper and stir through the garlic.

Once the bouillabaisse is cooked, remove from the heat and stir through the beans. Serve topped with baked fennel, a dollop of aïoli and a sprinkling of herbs, orange zest and seasoning, along with toast on the side.

Spreads and Sides

We have got superheroes living in our kitchen.

I am not talking about the Pippi Longstocking doll or Spiderman figure that both have the magical ability to always end up on the kitchen floor regardless of how many times we pick them up.

No, our superheroes live in jars. Some are creamy, rich and smooth, others are tangy and intense; we have the sweet and spicy and also the roasted crunchy. I'm talking about all our jars filled with nut butters, bean or vegetable spreads, spice blends, sprouts, pickles and sauerkrauts. A dollop, a sprinkling or a spoonful of any of these on top of a dish has the magical power to take it from very good to spectacularly yummy.

In contrast to our Fridge Favourites (pages 21–41), these don't make up meals on their own; instead we love placing them on the table as a flavour or texture complement. Or simply for dipping vegetable sticks or our Flaxseed Crackers (page 209) in them. *Luise*

Apricot and Tomato Chutney

Makes approx. 350 g
(12¼ oz/1½ cups)

Prep + cook time:
50 minutes

My mum is the chutney maker in the family. During the autumn she always cooks large batches of apple chutney that she hands out to friends and family. So, truth be told, we don't really have to make it ourselves very often.

We originally created this one as a topping for our vegan burgers, but it has proven itself useful as a side for many other dishes and is also an excellent add-in in our waffle sandwiches. I just hope Mum will approve. *David*

2 tbsp extra-virgin olive oil
1 red onion, peeled
1 clove garlic, peeled
½–1 fresh red chilli, seeded
1 tsp black mustard seeds
1 tsp cumin seeds
400 g (14 oz) vine tomatoes, removed from the vine

10 unsulphured dried apricot halves
2 tbsp red wine vinegar
1 tsp tamari or soy sauce
1 tbsp pure maple syrup
sea salt
1 handful (25 g/¾ oz) fresh coriander (cilantro), leaves picked

Heat the oil in a medium-sized saucepan on a medium-low heat. Finely chop the onion, garlic and chilli, transfer to the pan, add the spices and sauté for about 15 minutes or until the onion has softened.

Meanwhile, roughly chop the tomatoes and apricots and add them to the pan along with the vinegar, tamari or soy and maple syrup and season to taste with salt. Bring to the boil, reduce the heat and simmer for about 30 minutes or until the tomatoes and apricots are tender and the chutney has reduced, stirring from time to time so the chutney doesn't burn on the base of the pan. Remove from the heat, roughly chop the coriander, stir through and set aside to cool.

Store the chutney in the fridge in a sterilised sealable glass jar and it will keep, unopened, for about a month.

Savoury Granola – Salad's Best Friend

Makes approx. 500 g
(1 lb/4 cups)

Prep + cook time:
30 minutes

Say hello to your salad's new best friend. This jar of mustardy granola has become a total game-changer in our kitchen. And if you are like us, and often mix leftovers into quick salad bowls, you will soon realise its potential. The granola has the most delicious flavour, with heaps of mustard, orange zest, thyme and rosemary, and a pleasant crunch from buckwheat, nuts, seeds, rye and oats.

It adds a superb texture to all types of salads. It's also great with soups (perfect for gazpacho!) and on top of grilled feta or on a savoury yoghurt bowl.

DRY INGREDIENTS
2 tbsp fresh rosemary leaves or 1 tbsp dried rosemary leaves
2 tbsp fresh thyme leaves or 1 tbsp dried thyme leaves
75 g (2¾ oz/½ cup) hazelnuts
100 g (3½ oz/1 cup) rolled oats
100 g (3½ oz/1 cup) rye flakes
100 g (3½ oz/½ cup) raw buckwheat groats
70 g (2½ oz/½ cup) pumpkin seeds

70 g (2½ oz/½ cup) sunflower seeds
zest of 1 orange
sea salt and freshly ground black pepper

WET INGREDIENTS
120 ml (4 fl oz/½ cup) extra-virgin olive oil
2 tbsp wholegrain mustard
1 tbsp runny honey or pure maple syrup

Preheat the oven to 180°C (350°F/Gas mark 4) and line a baking tray with parchment paper.

Finely chop the herbs, transfer to a large mixing bowl and add the rest of the dry ingredients. Season to taste with salt and pepper, mix until combined and set aside while you prepare the wet ingredients.

Place all of the wet ingredients in a small bowl and whisk until combined. Pour the wet ingredients over the dry ingredients and, using your hands or a spatula, mix until well combined.

Spread the granola out in a single layer on the tray and bake for 15–20 minutes or until crunchy and golden. Stir it from time to time to prevent it from burning. Remove from the oven and set aside to cool completely.

Store the granola at room temperature in a large sealable glass jar and it will keep for a month or so.

TIPS:
For a nut-free alternative, replace the hazelnuts with more sunflower and pumpkin seeds.

You can of course add to or replace any of the seeds, nuts or flakes with what you have in your store cupboard. If you are looking for a slightly lighter granola, replace some of the oil with water.

Dukkah

Makes approx. 125 g
(4½ oz/1 cup)

Prep + cook time:
10 minutes

This nutty Middle Eastern spice mix adds both flavour and texture and is therefore ideal on so many vegetarian dishes. We love it on top of a sandwich, with roasted vegetables or sprinkled over a salad. We also always use it on top of our Herby Green Breakfast Bowl (page 50).

75 g (2¾ oz/½ cup) hazelnuts
3 tbsp coriander seeds
2 tbsp sunflower seeds
2 tbsp sesame seeds, colour of choice

1 tbsp cumin seeds
1 tbsp fennel seeds
1 tsp nigella seeds
½ tsp sea salt

TIP:
For a nut-free alternative, replace the hazelnuts with more sunflower, sesame and nigella seeds.

Place a large frying pan (skillet) on a medium-low heat. Finely chop the hazelnuts, transfer them to the dry pan, add the rest of the dukkah ingredients and sauté for about 5 minutes or until aromatic and golden, stirring from time to time to prevent the spices and nuts from burning. Transfer to a mortar and pestle and crush until the texture resembles coarse breadcrumbs.

Store the dukkah at room temperature in a sealable glass jar and it will keep for 10–15 days.

Za'atar

Makes 600 g
(1 lb 5 oz/2 cups)

Prep + cook time:
10 minutes

This is another Middle Eastern spice blend. We shared this recipe in our second cookbook, *Green Kitchen Travels,* but we refer to it quite often, so we thought it could be handy here as well.

4 tbsp hulled sesame seeds
4 tbsp ground sumac
2 tbsp dried thyme

½ tbsp ground cumin (optional)
a pinch of sea salt

Toast the sesame seeds in a dry frying pan (skillet) on a low heat for about 5 minutes or until golden. Stir them every now and again to prevent them from burning. Remove from the heat and set aside to cool.

Put the seeds and the rest of the ingredients in a bowl and mix well.

Pour into a small sealable glass jar. The za'atar will keep for months in the store cupboard, if sealed.

Easy Nut Butter

Here is the quick method we use to make nut butter. Essentially, you just need nuts, salt and a food processor that you trust. When toasted nuts are mixed in a food processor they slowly release their natural oils and transform into a smooth butter that is amazing on top of breakfast bowls and in desserts.

Makes approx. 50 g
(1¾ oz/½ cup)

Prep + cook time:
35 minutes

TIPS:
Making nut butter can be quite tough on food processors and low-budget brands tend to overheat easily, so stay attentive and turn it off to let it cool down if it starts smelling burnt.

If you prefer a crunchier texture, add some chopped nuts towards the end of blending in the food processor.

600 g (1 lb 5 oz/4 cups) nuts of choice
(or a combination of nuts and
seeds)
¼ tsp sea salt

Preheat the oven to 150°C (300°F/Gas mark 2).

Spread the nuts out in a single layer on a baking tray and toast for 10–15 minutes or until golden. Remove from the oven and set aside to cool. Put the nuts and salt in a food processor and blend on a high speed for 10–20 minutes or until completely smooth. It will take some time before the ground nuts start releasing their oil, so don't give up too early. Stop and scrape down the sides with a spatula every now and again (this also helps prevent your food processor from overheating).

Pour into a sterilised medium-sized sealable glass jar, cool and store in the fridge. The nut butter will keep for a few weeks, if sealed.

Three Wild Fermented Krauts

Makes approx. 1.5 kg
(3 lb 5 oz/6 cups)

Prep + cook time:
25 minutes +
2–4 weeks for the
krauts to ferment

Fermented foods are one of the healthiest things you can treat yourself to. They have been through a process called lacto fermentation in which bacteria feeds off the sugar and starch in the food, creating lactic acid. It is a probiotic strain of bacteria that helps our gut stay balanced and healthy.

Yoghurt, kefir, kimchi, kombucha, tempeh and sauerkraut are all types of fermented foods. One of our absolute favourites is sauerkraut. Regardless of its health advantages, we make and eat it because it tastes so good. It has a mildly acidic tanginess and freshness and adds a flavour punch to whatever we pair it with.

There are many ways to start a fermentation, but the easiest and most genuine is called wild fermentation and you only need two ingredients for it – cabbage and salt.

We learnt this process from two wonderful women in Bondi, Australia. Brenda and Vivianne run a small sauerkraut company there and they taught us how to make the Golden Sauerkraut that we are sharing here. From that recipe, we experimented with other flavourings. The golden one is very spicy and flavourful with anti-inflammatory ingredients. The green is bright and fresh and the ruby red is holiday-flavoured with tones of clove and cinnamon.

Use organic vegetables for fermenting and don't wash or scrub them too much, as this can destroy the natural enzymes on the vegetables.

Golden Sauerkraut

1.4 kg (3 lb) green cabbage, trimmed
and 2 outer leaves set aside for
sealing
3 carrots, tops removed and peeled
2 cloves of garlic, peeled
1½ tbsp ground turmeric
1 tbsp sea salt

1 tbsp peeled and grated fresh ginger
½ tbsp peeled and grated fresh
turmeric (optional)
½ tbsp caraway seeds
½ tbsp fennel seeds

Green Cabbage, Fennel and Apple Sauerkraut

1.4 kg (3 lb) green cabbage, trimmed
  and 2 outer leaves set aside for
  sealing
1 fennel bulb, stalks and fronds
  removed

1 onion, peeled
2 apples, cored
1 tbsp sea salt
1 tsp fennel seeds

Ruby Red Holiday Sauerkraut

1.4 kg (3 lb) red cabbage, trimmed and
  2 outer leaves set aside for sealing
1 red onion, peeled
400 g (14 oz) raw beetroots (beets),
  tops removed and peeled
1 tbsp sea salt

3 star anise
1 tsp whole cloves
1 tsp ground cinnamon
½ tsp whole black peppercorns
¼ tsp cardamom seeds

TIPS:
Alternatively, instead of slicing the vegetables, use a food processor with a slicing or shredding attachment.

We usually divide the fermented vegetables between smaller sterilised jars to give to friends and family or keep in the fridge.

While fermenting, some of the juice might leak through the lid and this can smell quite unpleasant. If this happens, place the jars in a bowl inside a plastic bag and close it. Then place in a cupboard and drain the leaked juices after about 3 days.

If the top is discoloured or has a bit of mould, don't be alarmed – just remove it and wipe around with a clean cloth or just change the jars.

Before you start: For each of these recipes you will need 1 large sterilised jar, or 2 smaller jars. To sterilise your jar(s), preheat the oven to 180°C (350°F/Gas mark 4), remove the rubber ring from the lid and place the jar(s) in a pan of boiling water for 10 minutes. Drain and place the jar(s) in the oven for 10 minutes to dry. Soak the rubber ring in hot water for a couple of minutes and dry thoroughly.

Thinly slice the cabbage, fennel or onion, grate the carrots, apples or beetroot and finely chop the garlic. Transfer to a large mixing bowl and add the rest of the ingredients.

Using your hands (it pays to wear disposable rubber gloves to prevent your hands from staining), mix and massage the vegetables intensely for about 10 minutes, until they are tender and very juicy. You may need to add more salt if the vegetables don't release enough juices. How much juice they release will depend on the season and how fresh the produce is.

Pack the sauerkraut tightly into one or two sterilised sealable glass jars, cover with the juices, top with the reserved cabbage leaves and seal.

Store the sauerkraut at room temperature out of direct sunlight for 2–4 weeks or until the veggies have fermented. When ready, the kraut should be softly textured but not mushy and have a fresh, spicy and acidic flavour. Remove the cabbage leaves and store in the fridge. It will keep for a few months.

Flaxseed Crackers

Makes 1 large oven tray
of crackers

Prep + cook time:
2 hours 30 minutes
+ 1 hour for the seeds
to soak

These crunchy little crackers are magically only made from seeds and water, which makes them both super-easy and the opposite of unhealthy. We usually put them on the table with some hummus or beetroot (beet) spread, but they are great with a slice of cheese on top as well.

When baking them, it is essential to spread the seed gel very, very thinly and then bake them for long enough so they crisp up without being burnt. We simply season them with salt and fennel seeds, but (almost) anything in the spice cabinet can be used.

110 g (3¾ oz/¾ cup) flaxseeds,
   colour of choice
40 g (1½ oz/¼ cup) chia seeds,
   colour of choice
1 tsp fennel seeds or seeds
   of choice
1 tsp sea salt

Place the seeds and salt in a medium-sized bowl, cover with 360 ml (12 fl oz/ 1½ cups) of water and mix until combined. Set aside to soak for 1 hour so that the seeds bind together to form a gel.

Preheat the oven to 100°c (200°F/Gas mark 1) and line a baking tray with parchment paper. Pour the seed gel onto the tray and, using a spatula or your hands, spread the gel out into a thin and even layer to cover the entire surface of the tray. Bake for about 2½ hours or until golden and crispy.

Remove from the oven, turn the tray upside down and carefully remove the parchment paper. Allow to cool completely on a wire rack before breaking up into smaller pieces.

Store the crackers at room temperature in an airtight container and they will keep for about 1 week.

Beetroot Spread

Makes 500 g (1 lb/4 cups)

Prep + cook time:
10 minutes

This simple spread has a truly unique flavour profile and that also makes it a tad difficult to describe. It hits notes all over the flavour map – earthy and sweet beetroot, rich avocado, tangy lemon, salty capers and peppery Dijon mustard – and that makes it very useful. We dollop it on top of our Burrata, Peach and Grilled Vegetable Salad (page 161), but we also enjoy it with Roasted Roots and Veg (page 35), our #GKS Bowl (page 111) or inside a waffle toastie (see our Roasted Root and Rye Waffle Toastie on page 140).

Its key feature is simplicity. No cooking is required. All the ingredients are simply mixed together in a food processor.

500 g (1 lb) raw beetroots (beets), trimmed, tops removed and peeled
2 ripe avocados, stones removed and flesh scooped out
zest and juice of 1 unwaxed lemon
2 tbsp pickled capers, drained and rinsed
1 tbsp Dijon mustard
sea salt and freshly ground black pepper

Grate the beetroot, transfer to a food processor or blender and add the rest of the ingredients. Season to taste with salt and pepper and blend until well combined.

Store the beetroot spread in the fridge in a sealable glass jar and it will keep for 4–5 days.

TIP:
Alternatively, prepare the beetroot (beet) spread in a medium-sized bowl with an immersion (hand) blender.

Desserts

Baking and experimenting with sweet treats has always had a deeply joyful effect on me. I guess it is partly connected with the anticipation that something delicious is en route but it's also the process that excites me. The toasting of the nuts, melting of the butter, the way a few sea salt flakes enhance the chocolate flavour, how natural syrups can be extracted from a fruit by macerating it in honey and lemon. And, of course, the smell that finds its way through our kitchen when a cake is in the oven. It's pure happiness.

I have been baking since I was a kid and still remember the recipes for the blueberry muffins and sticky chocolate cake that I used to bake with my mum. Luise's and my dessert recipes, however, have new qualities to them. We use natural sweeteners that often bring a wonderful flavour of their own to the desserts – burnt tones of maple syrup, flowery hints from honey, caramel nuances in soft dates and all that wide fruitiness from bananas. By incorporating nut flours in our baked recipes we add interesting texture, flavour and moisture to them. We also feature pumpkin, beetroot (beet), avocado and even black beans in some of our recipes – sometimes because of the colour and flavour that they add, other times because they have the perfect texture.

Our intention has never been to create anything less tasty or indulgent than you are used to. Quite the opposite: we have taken these off-path routes to bring more natural flavours, sweetness and hidden tones to our desserts, which make them both more interesting and lip-smackingly delicious. *David*

Baked Va-va-voom Doughnuts

Makes 12 doughnuts

Prep + cook time:
35 minutes

We are not too obsessed with special gear and gadgets in our kitchen, but the simple non-stick doughnut pan that we came across a couple of years ago has become immensely popular, especially with our kids.

Doughnuts have always been one of the ultimate naughty treats as they are not only deep-fried but also covered and infused with absurd amounts of sugar. But, using our doughnut pan, we make a version that is lighter, a lot less greasy, much quicker and still super-tasty and indulgent. Win! One of the secrets behind a tasty baked doughnut is not to over-bake it, as you want the consistency to almost melt in your mouth when you try a bite straight from the oven.

They are great on their own, but there are a number of different toppings that add even more va-va-voom to them. Some days we simply drizzle melted dark chocolate over them and other days we toss them in cinnamon sugar. My personal favourite, however, is the black version with liquorice powder! *David*

DRY INGREDIENTS
150 g (5¼ oz/1 cup) rice flour (or spelt flour)
100 g (3½ oz/1 cup) almond flour
50 g (1¾ oz/½ cup) desiccated unsweetened coconut
2 tsp baking powder
1 tsp ground cinnamon
½ tsp ground vanilla or 1 tsp vanilla extract
a pinch of sea salt

WET INGREDIENTS
14 soft dates, pitted
250 ml (8 fl oz/1 cup) full-fat plain unsweetened yoghurt
3 free-range eggs
5 tbsp virgin coconut oil or butter, melted
3 tbsp pure maple syrup

DARK CHOCOLATE TOPPING
60 g (2 oz) good-quality dark chocolate (at least 70% cocoa solids)

COCONUT SUGAR TOPPING
4 tbsp coconut or turbinado sugar
2 tbsp ground cinnamon or liquorice root powder or pink mineral glitter
5 tbsp virgin coconut oil or butter, melted

TIPS:
If you can't find soft dates, soak dried dates in hot water for 20 minutes.

Bake them as muffins if you don't have a doughnut tin.

For a nut-free alternative, replace the almond flour with pumpkin seed, sunflower seed or linseed flour.

continues overleaf

Preheat the oven to 200°C (400°F/Gas mark 6) and grease a 12-hole doughnut tin (or two 6-hole ones).

Place all of the dry ingredients in a large mixing bowl and stir until combined. Make a well in the centre and set aside while you prepare the wet ingredients.

Mash the dates with a fork and place them in a food processor along with the rest of the wet ingredients. Blend until smooth, then pour into the well of the dry ingredients. Using a spatula, gently fold the wet ingredients into the dry ingredients until just combined, making sure not to over-mix or the doughnuts will be tough. Spoon the batter into the doughnut moulds until flush with the top of the tin.

Bake for 12–15 minutes or until golden and puffed. Remove from the oven and set aside to cool slightly in the tin then transfer to a wire rack to cool completely or devour them plain while still warm.

For the dark chocolate topping, melt the chocolate in a bain-marie or water bath then drizzle over the doughnuts.

For the coconut sugar topping, place the sugar and cinnamon or liquorice root powder in a plastic bag, dunk each doughnut in the oil, transfer to the bag and shake until well coated.

Beetroot Crêpes with Warm Blueberry Compote and Yoghurt

Adding beetroot (beet) to our crêpe batter gives it a mildly sweet and earthy undertone and – more importantly – a gorgeous pink/red/purple colour.

Here, we serve the crêpes as dessert. We top them with a cardamom-flavoured blueberry compote, fresh berries and a dollop of yoghurt. We have halved our Rice Crêpe Batter (page 32) as you probably don't need more for dessert, but you can make the full recipe and serve the first crêpes with a savoury filling and the last ones with a sweet: that is how we usually do it.

½ batch Rice Crêpe Batter (page 32)
30 g (1 oz) raw beetroot (beet),
   trimmed, tops removed and peeled
¼ tsp ground vanilla or 1 tsp vanilla
   extract
virgin coconut oil or butter, to fry

BLUEBERRY COMPOTE
150 g (5¼ oz/1 cup) blueberries, fresh
   or frozen
1 tbsp lemon juice

2 tsp pure maple syrup
1 tsp ground cardamom
¼ tsp ground vanilla or 1 tsp vanilla
   extract

TO SERVE
fresh berries of choice
full-fat plain unsweetened yoghurt
   of choice
slivered almonds
torn fresh mint or lemon balm leaves

Place the crêpe batter in a blender or food processor. Grate the beetroot, transfer to the blender along with the vanilla, blend until completely smooth and pink.

To prepare the warm blueberry compote, place all of the ingredients in a small saucepan, bring to a gentle boil, reduce the heat and simmer for about 5 minutes or until warm and reduced. Set aside while you cook the crêpes.

Heat a little oil in a 20 cm (8 inch) non-stick frying pan (skillet) on a medium-high heat. Once hot, whisk the batter then ladle 80 ml (2½ fl oz/⅓ cup) into the pan, tilting the pan to spread and evenly distribute the batter.

Fry for 1–2 minutes or until small bubbles form on the surface and the base is golden. Carefully flip the crêpe with a spatula and fry the other side for a further 1–2 minutes or until cooked and golden. Transfer to a plate and repeat with the rest of the batter (you may need to reduce the heat slightly after the first crêpe).

Serve topped with some compote, berries, a dollop of yoghurt, slivered almonds and a scattering of mint or lemon balm.

Banana Nice Cream with Peanut Butter 'Cookie Dough'

Serves 4

Prep + cook time:
15 minutes

Banana 'nice cream' must be the easiest ice cream ever invented as it only calls for ONE ingredient. And if you have bananas in your freezer it is just a two-minute job to mix them up into a luscious creamy soft-serve. To make this treat even better, we often mix the nice cream with a quick and easy 'cookie dough' made of peanut butter and dates. It is the ultimate speedy dessert that we can whip up without having to take a trip to the supermarket. There are endless ways to make your nice cream even more luxurious, by adding various toppings, fruit, jams or mix-ins.

'COOKIE DOUGH'
2 tbsp pea or Easy Nut Butter
 (page 203)
3 soft dates, pitted
1 tbsp buckwheat flour or flour
 of choice
a pinch of sea salt

BANANA NICE CREAM
4 frozen bananas, peeled and sliced
50 g (1¾ oz) good-quality dark
 chocolate (at least 70% cocoa
 solids) or 4 tbsp cacao nibs

Prepare the 'cookie dough' by placing all of the ingredients plus a tablespoon of water in a food processor or blender and blending until the texture resembles cookie dough. Transfer to a flat surface and, using your hands, roll into one long log about 30 cm (12 inches) long and 1 cm (½ inch) in diameter. Cut into 5 mm (⅛ inch) thick pieces and set aside while you finish the nice cream.

Place the frozen banana slices in a food processor or blender and blend until smooth, thick and creamy. If your blender isn't strong enough, let the bananas sit for about 10 minutes or until slightly defrosted and then try again.

Roughly chop the chocolate and add to the blender together with the cookie dough pieces. Pulse briefly once or twice and then serve the nice cream scooped into bowls or on waffles.

TIPS:
If you can't find soft dates, soak dried dates in hot water for 20 minutes.

For a nut-free alternative, replace the nut butter with a sunflower seed butter.

Warm Fruit Salad with Chocolate and Almonds

Serves 4

Prep + cook time:
20 minutes

This little gem is simple but brilliant. Giving the fruit salad a quick tour in the oven elevates the flavours, brings out the juices and melts the dark chocolate on top. It's such a simple dessert to throw together if you have friends over, and it feels a whole lot more exciting than a plain old platter of fruit.

It's a popular Swedish dessert that is normally made with white chocolate. We make it with dark chocolate, salted nuts and flaked coconut for extra crunch and goodness. Adapt the choice of fruit to the season.

1 tsp sea salt
100 g (3½ oz/¾ cup) almonds*
2 ripe bananas, peeled
3 kiwi fruits, peeled
3 fresh apricots, stones removed
2 plums, stones removed
10 fresh strawberries, tops removed
10 fresh cherries, stems removed
   and pitted

juice and zest of 1 lime
50 g (1¾ oz) good-quality dark
   chocolate (70% cocoa solids)
30 g (1 oz/⅓ cup) flaked coconut
   (coconut chips)

TO SERVE
full-fat plain unsweetened yoghurt
   of choice

As a shortcut, simply use store-bought salted almonds but omit the water and salt.

TIPS:
For a nut-free alternative, replace the almonds with sunflower or pumpkin seeds.

For a vegan alternative, replace the yoghurt with a plant-based yoghurt such as coconut or soy.

Preheat the oven to 200°C (400°F/Gas mark 6) and line a baking tray with parchment paper.

Place 1 tablespoon of boiled water and the salt in a medium-sized mixing bowl and stir until dissolved. Add the almonds and mix until combined. Transfer the almonds to the baking tray and bake for about 10 minutes or until lightly toasted. Remove from the oven and set aside.

Meanwhile, prepare the fruit salad. Cut the fruit into bite-sized pieces and transfer to a baking dish. Drizzle over the lime juice and toss until well coated. Roughly chop the salted almonds and sprinkle them over the fruit salad. Grate over the chocolate then scatter the flaked coconut and lime zest on top.

Bake for 7–8 minutes or until the fruit is warm and juicy, the chocolate has melted and the flaked coconut is golden.

Serve topped with a dollop of yoghurt.

Nutty Quinoa and Chocolate Bars

Every time David makes these bars he has the annoying habit of cutting each one in half. His theory is that they will last longer. Of course they don't. They are too good for me to settle for half a bar so I just take two pieces every time I visit the freezer. They are decadently sweet, addictive, energising and rich with a fresh punch from the ginger. We usually top it with coconut but freeze-dried berries are also beautiful. Enjoy them as a midday snack, post-workout fuel or a weekday dessert. *Luise*

Makes 12 bars

Prep + cook time:
20 minutes +
1 hour to chill

2 tbsp virgin coconut oil, plus extra
    to grease
10 soft dates, pitted
250 ml (8 fl oz/1 cup) crunchy peanut
    butter or Easy Nut Butter of choice
    (page 203) or peanut butter
1 tbsp fresh ginger, peeled and grated
75 g (2¾ oz/½ cup) pumpkin seeds
    or seeds of choice, toasted

40 g (1½ oz/¼ cup) almonds
30 g (1 oz/1 cup) puffed quinoa
a pinch of sea salt (optional)

CHOCOLATE TOPPING
100 g (3½ oz) good-quality dark
    chocolate (at least 70% cocoa
    solids)
25 g (¾ oz/¼ cup) desiccated
    unsweetened coconut

TIPS:
Puffed quinoa can be found in health food stores but if you have difficulties finding it, try using puffed amaranth, puffed rice, puffed buckwheat or cornflakes, or simply add more nuts and seeds.

If you can't find soft dates, soak dried dates in hot water for 20 minutes.

You can make your own chocolate by melting 2 tbsp coconut oil and 2 tbsp maple syrup in a small saucepan on a low heat. Sift in 2 tbsp cacao powder and stir until silky smooth.

For a nut-free alternative, replace the peanut butter with a seed butter of choice and replace the almonds with sunflower seeds.

Grease a 15 × 20 cm (6 × 8 inch) baking tin or line it with parchment paper.

Melt the oil in a medium-sized saucepan on a low heat. Mash the dates with a fork and add them to the pan along with the nut butter and ginger. Stir for a few minutes until combined, remove from the heat and set aside. Roughly chop the pumpkin seeds and almonds and add them to the pan along with the puffed quinoa and salt (if using). Stir until well combined.

Transfer to the baking tin and, using the palm of your hand or the back of a spoon (coated in coconut oil), press the mixture down firmly to create an even and compact bar. Place in the freezer while you prepare the chocolate topping.

Melt the the chocolate in a bain-marie or in a small bowl placed over a saucepan with boiling water. Remove the baking tin from the freezer and pour the melted chocolate over the bar. Tap the tin lightly on the bench to smooth out the surface. Leave for a few minutes and when it begins to set, sprinkle over the coconut.

Put the tin back in the freezer for 1 hour then remove and slice into 5 × 5 cm (2 × 2 inch) bars. They will keep for a few months stored in the freezer in an airtight container. Thaw them slightly before serving – they're best when cold!

Berry, Rhubarb and Date Crumble

Serves 8

Prep + cook time:
40 minutes

Few things are more salivating than the sizzling sound of fruit juices bubbling in the oven, combined with the scent of fruit, almond and vanilla.

This is the crumble recipe we build from every time. It is vegan and gluten-free and is therefore a safe card regardless of allergies and preferences.

We combine rolled oats with quinoa flakes, which are sturdier and add a nice crunch. Adding soft dates to the crumble topping to make it sweet and chunky.

Depending on preference and the tartness of the fruit and berries, you can add more sweetener to the fruit or crumble topping.

FRUIT FILLING
8 thin rhubarb stalks (approx 150 g/ 5¼ oz) , trimmed and tops removed (or 2 more cups of berries)
300 g (10½ oz/2 cups) berries of choice, fresh or frozen
1 tbsp pure maple syrup, runny honey or brown rice syrup
juice of ½ lemon
½ tsp ground vanilla or 2 tsp vanilla extract

CRUMBLE TOPPING
100 g (3½ oz/1 cup) rolled oats
100 g (3½ oz/1 cup) quinoa flakes (or 1 more cup of rolled oats)
40 g (1½ oz/ ⅓ cup) almond flour
¼ tsp sea salt
15 soft dates, pitted
125 g (4½ oz/½ cup) virgin coconut oil, solidified, or 125 g (4½ oz) butter, cubed and chilled

TO SERVE
full-fat plain yoghurt

Preheat the oven to 180°C (350°F/Gas mark 4) and grease a 20 cm (8 inch) baking dish or pie tin. Cut the rhubarb into small pieces, transfer to the dish and add the berries. Drizzle over the syrup, lemon juice and vanilla and toss until well coated.

To prepare the crumble topping, place the oats, quinoa, almond flour and salt in a medium-sized mixing bowl and mix until combined. Mash the dates with a fork and add them to the bowl along with the coconut oil. Using your hands, rub the dates and oil into the dry ingredients until the texture resembles coarse crumbs or clusters.

Top the fruit with the crumble and bake for about 30 minutes or until the crumble topping is golden and the filling bubbles up around the edges. Serve warm topped with a dollop of yoghurt. Store the cooled crumble in the fridge in an airtight container and it will keep for 3–5 days.

TIPS:
For a nut-free alternative, replace the almond flour with pumpkin seed, sunflower seed or linseed flour.

If you can't find soft dates, soak dried dates in hot water for 20 minutes.

Buckwheat, Banana and Chocolate Bread

Makes approx. 12 slices

Prep + cook time: 50 minutes

This grown-up version of the classic banana bread with chocolate and tones of coffee is a true family favourite. It has a wonderfully moist texture and is pleasantly decadent without being too sweet (it is called bread, after all). We sometimes add a hidden layer of either dark chocolate or walnuts to the middle of the cake. Baked goods are always best enjoyed warm from the oven but this bread tastes really good also on day 2 and 3.

2 free-range eggs
70 g (2½ oz/½ heaping cup) coconut sugar or turbinado sugar
3 small/medium ripe bananas, peeled
120 ml (4 fl oz/½ cup) mildly flavoured rapeseed oil
1 tablespoon coffee (optional)
100 g (3½ oz/1 cup) almond flour
120 g (4¼ oz/1 cup) buckwheat flour
5 tablespoons cacao powder
1 teaspoon baking powder
1 pinch sea salt

FILLING
50 g (1¾ oz) good-quality dark chocolate (70% cocoa solids) or walnuts (optional)

TOPPING
1 ripe banana, peeled
oil, for brushing
1 teaspoon roasted coffee beans, coarsely ground (optional)

Preheat the oven to 180°C (350°F/Gas mark 4) and line a 10 × 25 cm (4 × 10 inch) loaf tin with parchment paper.

Crack the eggs into a food processor, add the sugar, break in the bananas, the oil and the coffee and mix on high speed until smooth. Add the flours and the rest of the loaf ingredients and pulse until just combined, making sure not to over-mix or the loaf will be compact.

Pour half of the batter into the tin, roughly chop the chocolate or walnuts (if using), scatter on top and cover with the rest of the batter. Cut the banana in half lengthwise, arrange the two halves cut side up on top of the batter, brush the bananas with a little oil and sprinkle coffee beans on top.

Bake for about 35–45 minutes or until a skewer inserted in the centre of the loaf comes out clean. Remove from the oven and set aside to cool slightly in the tin before devouring it while still warm. Store the loaf at room temperature in an airtight container and it will keep for 3–5 days. Alternatively, pre-slice and freeze it (and then toast the frozen slices).

TIPS:
For a nut-free version, replace the almond flour with oat flour and skip the walnuts in the middle.

If you don't have a food processor, crack the eggs into a medium size mixing-bowl and whisk together with the sugar. Mash the bananas with a fork, and add to the bowl along with the oil. Whisk until smooth. Then add the rest of the loaf ingredients and stir until just combined.

Rhubarb and Chia Parfait

Serves 4

Prep + cook time:
10 minutes

If we could include scratch-and-sniff pages in our book, this would easily become the most frequently cooked recipe. The smell of melted butter, honey, rhubarb, ginger, cardamom and nuts frying in the pan is addictive. It's a true last-minute dessert as you can whip it together in 10 minutes (if you have the cold ingredients ready in the fridge).

We adapt this recipe with whatever seasonal ingredients are available: plums, peaches, pineapple, berries, apples or pears can be used instead of rhubarb. It's easily made vegan by using coconut yoghurt or a GMO-free soy yoghurt.

2 tbsp virgin coconut oil, butter
   or ghee
2 tbsp pure maple syrup, runny honey
   or brown rice syrup
2 thin rhubarb stalks, trimmed and
   tops removed
50 g (1¾ oz/⅓ cup) hazelnuts
50 g (1¾ oz/⅓ cup) sunflower seeds
½ tsp ground ginger
½ tsp ground cardamom
a pinch of sea salt

TO SERVE
½ batch (250 ml/8 fl oz/1 cup)
   Chia to Share (page 41)
Easy Nut Butter of choice (page 203)
full-fat plain unsweetened yoghurt
   or coconut yoghurt
pure maple syrup or runny honey

Make sure you have half a batch of Chia to share in the fridge. If not, start by making one.

Heat the oil and maple syrup in a medium-sized frying pan (skillet) on a medium heat. Cut the rhubarb into small pieces and roughly chop the hazelnuts. Transfer to the pan along with the seeds, spices and salt. Sauté for 5–8 minutes or until the rhubarb is tender and the nuts and seeds are golden and toasted.

To assemble the parfait, place a few spoonfuls of chia pudding in the bottom of four glasses. Serve topped with a dollop of nut butter, a few spoonfuls of yoghurt, the warm rhubarb and nut topping and a drizzle of maple syrup.

TIP:
For a nut-free alternative, replace the hazelnuts with pumpkin seeds.

Shattered Blueberry and Yoghurt Cake

Serves 8

Prep + cook time:
1 hour + 30 minutes

No, we didn't accidentally drop this cake on the ground before serving it. We shattered it into pieces on purpose! We got the idea from a deconstructed chocolate cake we had at a Copenhagen rooftop restaurant a couple of years ago. By shattering the cake and layering the pieces with yoghurt and whipped cream it looks even more decadent and it also turns the serving process into a lottery, as the pieces come in all shapes and sizes. As spectacular as it might look, the great flavour and texture are actually our favourite things about this cake. Light, moist and sweet, with pieces of blueberries breaking through.

We use this cake as a standard birthday cake in our family. For our daughter Elsa's 6th birthday we omitted the berries, doubled the recipe and shaped the cake as a fairy (obviously not shattered!).

DRY INGREDIENTS
100 g (3½ oz/1 cup) rolled oats
100 g (3½ oz/1 cup) almond flour
80 g (3 oz/½ cup) rice flour
1 tsp baking powder
½ tsp sea salt
¼ tsp ground vanilla
   or ½ tsp vanilla extract

WET INGREDIENTS
100 g (3½ oz) butter, at room
   temperature
160 ml (5½ fl oz/⅔ cup) pure maple
   syrup or runny honey

WET INGREDIENTS (cont.)
zest of 1 unwaxed lemon
250 ml (8 fl oz/1 cup) full-fat plain
   unsweetened yoghurt
3 free-range eggs, separated
300 g (10½ oz/2 cups) blueberries
   or berries of choice, fresh or frozen
   (thawed)

TO SERVE
full-fat plain unsweetened yoghurt
whipped cream
fresh berries of choice

Preheat the oven to 180°C (350°F/Gas mark 4), grease a 20 cm (8 inch) springform cake tin and line it with parchment paper.

Place the oats in a food processor and blend until the texture resembles coarse flour. Transfer to a large mixing bowl, add the rest of the dry ingredients and stir until combined. Make a well in the centre and set aside while you prepare the wet ingredients.

continues overleaf

the maple syrup and lemon zest and mix until well combined and creamy. Add the yoghurt and egg yolks, mix until just combined and set aside.

Place the egg whites in a clean, dry bowl of the stand mixer or in a medium-sized mixing bowl and beat until soft peaks form. Using a spatula, gently fold the wet ingredients, followed by the egg whites and half the blueberries, into the dry ingredients until just combined, making sure not to over-mix as the cake will be compact otherwise.

Pour the cake batter into the tin, scatter the remaining blueberries on top and bake for about 1 hour or until golden and a skewer inserted in the centre of the cake comes out clean. Remove from the oven and set aside to cool slightly in the tin before transferring to a wire rack to cool completely. Store the cake at room temperature in an airtight container and it will keep for 3–5 days.

When ready to serve, carefully break the cake up into different-sized pieces and separate them slightly, while still maintaining the overall circular shape of the cake. Serve topped with dollops of yoghurt, cream and a scattering of berries.

Black Bean Mocha Mousse Cake

Serves 12

Prep + cook time:
25 minutes +
4 hours to freeze

May we suggest that you don't reveal the ingredients in this cake before serving it? People have a tendency of putting their prejudices first, and it would be a shame if that hindered them from tasting this lusciously smooth, creamy and delicious cake with plenty of nuts, coffee and chocolate. Yes, there is a whole tin of black beans in the filling, but it doesn't affect the flavour. Instead, it adds body to the cake (as well as making it more nutritious than a standard mousse cake).

Serve it frozen, like an ice-cream cake, or thawed, as a mousse cake, with fresh cherries, toasted hazelnuts and a dark chocolate drizzle on top.

BASE
150 g (5¼ oz/1 cup) hazelnuts, toasted
10 large soft dates, pitted
3 tbsp raw cacao powder
1 tbsp virgin coconut oil
a pinch of sea salt

FILLING
80 ml (2½ fl oz/⅓ cup) plant-based milk of choice
100 g (3½ oz) good-quality dark chocolate (70% cocoa solids)
1 × 400 g (14 oz) tin black beans,* drained and rinsed

FILLING (cont.)
5 large soft dates, pitted
1 tbsp virgin coconut oil
4 tbsp (2 shots) espresso

TOPPING
50 g (1¾ oz) good-quality dark chocolate (70% cocoa solids), melted
75 g (2¾ oz/½ cup) hazelnuts, toasted
4 tbsp roasted coffee beans

TO SERVE
fresh cherries or berries of choice

Grease a 20 cm (8 inch) springform cake tin and line it with parchment paper.

Place the hazelnuts in a food processor and pulse until roughly chopped. Add the rest of the base ingredients to the food processor and blend until the mixture resembles coarse breadcrumbs and holds together when pinched. Transfer to the tin and, using the palm of your hand or the back of a spoon, press the mixture down firmly to create an even and compact base. Transfer to the freezer.

To prepare the filling, heat the milk in a small stainless-steel mixing bowl over a small saucepan of simmering water. Break the chocolate up and add it to the milk. Stir until the chocolate has nearly melted, then remove from the heat and stir until the chocolate has completely melted. Set aside.

Place the beans, dates, oil and coffee in the food processor and blend on a high

* or 200 g/7 oz/1½ cups cooked black beans

TIP:
If you can't find soft dates, soak dried dates in hot water for 20 minutes.

speed until completely smooth. Add the melted chocolate and blend again on a high speed until silky smooth.

Remove the tin from the freezer and pour the filling over the base. Tap the tin lightly on the bench to smooth out the surface. Return to the freezer to set for at least 4 hours (or overnight) until completely firm.

Once set, remove from the freezer and from the cake tin and drizzle with the chocolate. Roughly chop the hazelnuts and scatter on top along with the coffee beans. Leave to thaw for about 30 minutes then cut the cake with a sharp knife dipped in hot water.

Serve with fresh cherries or berries.

Store the cake slices in the freezer in an airtight container and they will keep for a few months (even though you know they won't!). Just remember to thaw them before serving.

Oat and Ginger Thins

Thin and crispy, perfectly sweet with a distinct oat and butter flavour and hints of ginger and clove, this is our daughter's favourite cookie recipe. Probably because it is so insanely quick to make that she can help me prepare it before something more exciting steals her attention. I love it too. It has a short ingredient list and we almost always have its components at home. Most of the time we eat them straight from the baking tray, but they are also delicious sandwiched around a scoop of the Banana Nice Cream recipe on page 221. *David*

DRY INGREDIENTS
200 g (7 oz/2 cups) rolled oats
4 tbsp buckwheat flour
1½ tsp ground ginger
½ tsp ground vanilla or
    1 tsp vanilla extract
½ tsp sea salt
a pinch of ground cloves

WET INGREDIENTS
8 tbsp virgin coconut oil, solidified,
    or 120 g (4¼ oz) butter cubed
    and chilled
6 tbsp pure maple syrup or runny
    honey
4 tbsp plant-based milk
    of choice

TO SERVE
Banana Nice Cream (page 221)
    or ice cream (optional)

Preheat the oven to 180°C (350°F/Gas mark 4) and line a baking tray with parchment paper.

Place all of the dry ingredients in a large mixing bowl and mix until combined. Add all of the wet ingredients and, using your hands, rub the oil into the dry ingredients until the texture resembles coarse breadcrumbs.

Divide the dough into 20 pieces and shape them into little balls with your hands. Transfer to the tray and press them down into flat discs about 7 cm (2¾ inches) in diameter and 5 mm (⅛ inch) thick and bake for about 15 minutes or until golden and crispy. Remove from the oven and set aside to cool completely on a wire rack.

Serve as they are, or with ice cream sandwiched in between 2 oat thins.

Store the oat thins at room temperature in an airtight container and they will keep for 3–5 days.

Italian Cheesecake Jars

Serves 4

Prep + cook time:
25 minutes

This is the kind of thing we make in the middle of the summer when we crave dessert but don't feel like pulling out any mixers or turning on the oven. It is almost too simple and perfect for summer parties. It features two of our favourite summer fruits on a bed of creamy lemon and vanilla mascarpone and the simplest raw crumble you'll ever make. The fruit is macerated in lemon juice and honey, which increases the flavour and brings out some of the fruit juices. If strawberries and peaches are not in season, use other seasonal fruit.

TOPPING
16 fresh strawberries, tops removed
2 ripe peaches, stones removed
1 tbsp runny honey or pure maple
    syrup
juice of ½ lemon

BASE
75 g (2¾ oz/½ cup) almonds
8 soft dates, pitted
a pinch of flaky sea salt

FILLING
250 g (8¾ oz/1 cup) mascarpone
1–2 tbsp runny honey or pure
    maple syrup
zest of 1 unwaxed lemon
juice of ½ lemon
½ tsp ground vanilla or
    2 tsp vanilla extract

TO SERVE
torn fresh lemon balm or mint leaves
elderflower or lavender petals
    (optional)

TIPS:
For a nut-free alternative, replace the almonds with sunflower seeds or pumpkin seeds.

For a lighter version, replace the mascarpone with regular yoghurt.

For a vegan alternative, replace the mascarpone with coconut yoghurt.

If you can't find soft dates, soak dried dates in hot water for 20 minutes.

To prepare the topping, cut the fruit into bite-sized pieces, transfer to a medium-sized mixing bowl, drizzle over the honey or syrup and lemon juice and toss until well coated. Set aside for about 15 minutes to macerate.

Meanwhile, prepare the base. Roughly chop the almonds and mash the dates with a fork. Transfer to a medium-sized mixing bowl. Add the salt and, using your hands, rub the dates into the almonds until combined. Set aside while you prepare the filling.

Place the mascarpone, honey or syrup, lemon zest and juice and vanilla in a medium-sized mixing bowl and mix until combined.

To assemble, crumble the almond and date mixture into the base of four jars, dollop the mascarpone filling on top and spoon over the fruit.

Serve topped with a sprinkling of lemon balm or mint, and elderflower or lavender petals (if you wish).

Pumpkin Pie Chocolate Bars

Makes 24 bars

Prep + cook time:
45 minutes + 3 hours
for the cashew nuts
to soak + 3 hours for
the bars to freeze

These are cute little sweets that we enjoy when pumpkins are in season. Most pumpkin recipes and sweets are served warm, but these are almost like ice-cream bars, which makes a nice contrast to the warm and sweet spices.

There is a thin layer of coconut in the bottom and the filling is a combination of pumpkin purée and our favourite date caramel recipe. It's seriously good!

It takes a little jiggling to cover the bar in chocolate and some waiting for the pumpkin layer to set, but apart from that, it is pretty straightforward. When eaten directly from the freezer it has a proper ice-cream texture, and when left an hour at room temperature the inside gets more caramel-like. The perfect texture is achieved somewhere in between.

BASE
100 g (3½ oz/1 cup) desiccated
    unsweetened coconut
8 soft dates, pitted
1 tbsp virgin coconut oil,
    plus extra to grease

FILLING
250 g (8¾ oz/1 cup) Pumpkin Purée
    (page 28)
75 g (2¾ oz/½ cup) cashew nuts,
    soaked in filtered water for 3 hours
    then strained and rinsed
10 soft dates, pitted

FILLING (cont.)
4 tbsp hulled tahini
4 tbsp virgin coconut oil
2 tbsp pure maple syrup
½ tsp ground cinnamon
½ tsp sea salt
¼ tsp ground ginger
a pinch of ground cloves

CHOCOLATE TOPPING*
300 g (10½ oz) good-quality dark
    chocolate (at least 70% cocoa
    solids)

*If you don't want to use
chocolate, substitute with
8 tbsp each of virgin coconut
oil, pure maple syrup and
raw cacao powder and follow
the method.*

TIPS:
*If you can't find soft dates,
soak dried dates in hot water
for 20 minutes.*

*For a nut-free alternative,
replace the cashew nuts with
cooked chickpeas (garbanzo
beans) (page 26).*

Grease a 20 × 20 cm (8 × 8 inch) baking tin and line it with parchment paper.

Place all of the base ingredients in a food processor and blend until the mixture resembles coarse breadcrumbs and holds together when pinched. Transfer to the tin and, using the palm of your hand or a spatula, press the mixture down firmly to create an even and compact base. Transfer to the freezer.

Place all of the filling ingredients, plus 6 tablespoons of water, in a blender or food processor and blend until completely smooth. Remove the tin from the freezer and spread the filling over the base. Tap the tin lightly on the bench to

continues overleaf

smooth out the surface. Return to the freezer to set for at least 3 hours
(or overnight) until completely firm.

Once set, remove from the freezer, slice into 2.5 × 5 cm (1 × 2 inch) bars and
return to the freezer while you prepare the topping. If using the dark chocolate,
melt in a bain-marie or water bath. If not, melt the oil with the maple syrup in a
small saucepan on a low heat. Sift in the cacao powder and stir until smooth.

Remove the bars from the freezer and line a flat dish with parchment paper.
Using a fork, dunk each bar into the melted chocolate, remove, letting the excess
chocolate drip away, transfer to the dish and return to the freezer to set.

If using homemade chocolate, add a second layer of coating by removing
the bars from the freezer once set, trim the chocolate edges and follow the
instructions of the previous step (store-bought chocolate only needs one coating).
Once set, remove the bars from the freezer, trim the chocolate edges and follow
the instructions of the previous step to coat the bars in a second layer of chocolate.

Store the bars in the freezer in an airtight container and they will keep for a
few months. Just remember to thaw them ever so slightly before serving –
they're best enjoyed cold.

Mango Sherbet with Chocolate-drizzled Pineapple

Serves 2

Prep + cook time:
15 minutes

This quick sherbet is a real explosion of fruity and tropical flavours, with lime and ginger to balance the sweet tones. It's a wonderful, cool treat on a warm day and it comes together in just a few minutes. Where we live, you can find frozen mango and avocado in the supermarket, but it's easy to make yourself: simply peel, chop and place in a container in the freezer. The chocolate-drizzled pineapple is popular with the kids. We try to keep a variety of chocolate-drizzled fruit in the freezer as a super-quick treat and here it doubles as a topping.

CHOCOLATE-DRIZZLED
PINEAPPLE
1 fresh pineapple, cored
60 g (2 oz) good-quality dark
    chocolate (at least 70%
    cocoa solids)
2 tbsp desiccated unsweetened
    coconut, toasted

SLUSH
250 g (8¾ oz/2 cups) frozen
    ripe mango
100 g (3½ oz/¾ cup) frozen avocado
juice of ½ orange
juice of ½ lime
1 tsp freshly grated ginger
1 tbsp pure maple syrup
2 passion fruits

TO SERVE
chopped almonds

Cut the pineapple into 1 cm (½ inch) thick slices and then cut them into triangles or half-moons. Lay them out on a sheet of parchment paper. Melt the chocolate in a bain-marie or water bath. Dip a spoon in the chocolate and drizzle it over the fruit. Sprinkle with the toasted coconut. Leave to set while you prepare the slush.

   Add the mango, avocado, orange juice, lime juice, ginger, maple syrup and the seeds from one of the passion fruits to a blender or food processor. Blend on a high speed until smooth, scraping down the sides if necessary. Divide the seeds from the second passion fruit between two glasses. Scoop the slush into the glasses, top with chocolate-drizzled pineapple and some chopped almonds. Serve immediately, with spoons.

Index

DAVID FRENKIEL and LUISE VINDAHL are the couple behind the award-winning vegetarian food blog *Green Kitchen Stories*, which has followers from all over the world. Healthy, seasonal and delicious vegetarian recipes paired with colourful and beautiful photographs have become the trademark of their style. They are also the authors of three internationally acclaimed cookbooks, *The Green Kitchen*, *Green Kitchen Travels* and *Green Kitchen Smoothies*, published by Hardie Grant UK.

David and Luise's work has appeared in *Food & Wine Magazine*, *Bon Appetit*, *ELLE*, *Vogue*, *The Guardian*, *Vegetarian Times* and many more publications. In 2013 and 2015 their blog was winner in the Saveur Magazine Best Food Blog Awards. They have released two best-selling apps for iPhone and iPad, which have been selected in the App Store Best of 2012, 2013 and 2014.

Luise is Danish and David is Swedish. They currently live in Stockholm with their daughter Elsa and sons Isac and Gabriel. Apart from doing freelance recipe development and food photography, David works as a freelance graphic designer and Luise is a qualified nutritional therapist.

Read more on www.greenkitchenstories.com

Acknowledgements

Writing and photographing a whole cookbook is a dream project. But doing it with the love of your life is also damn difficult and pretty complicated to say the least... Especially when you also have children together, who are running around your legs at every opportunity. In the final stages of production we always promise each other never to write another cookbook. But here we are, with a fourth book. And we still love each other. It's the biggest miracle of them all.

Luckily we have had two new people helping on the side this time, to give us perspective, feedback and relieve some of the worst stress. Thank you Nicola Moores for testing every single recipe in this book. Thank you for making them easier to understand, more consistent, for suggesting new recipe names when we have lost inspiration and for providing pages of pages of feedback. We are incredibly grateful for your commitment and impeccable sense for details.

Thank you also to Sophie Mackinnon for flying over here to assist us in the most intense part of the cookbook process. You didn't only help us to shop ingredients, write planning lists, prepare food during shoots and assist with the styling – but you also helped us to stay focused (and kind to each other). We really enjoyed our time together in a sunny Stockholm.

Thank you Kate Pollard, Stephen King and the rest of the gang at Hardie Grant for giving us the opportunity to write one more book. We really love working with all of you and are amazed by the trust and confidence you have showed in us.

Thank you Clare Skeats for designing this book and making it look so beautiful.

Thank you Brenda Boeder and Vivian Cordua from Raw Sisterhood for teaching us all about wild fermentation when we visited you in Bondi.

Thank you to our beloved families in Denmark and Sweden, for playing with the kids while we work on the weekends, for following us on this journey and for encouraging us in whatever steps we choose to take. We love you.

Thank you Elsa, Isac and baby Gabriel, who was born right before this book was sent to print. You are our true recipe testers and satisfying your taste buds will always be our biggest challenge and motivation. We are sorry for serving you reheated cookbook leftovers so many times a week. That stops now!

Finally, a massive thank you to all the readers of our blog, Green Kitchen Stories. Without your support, we wouldn't have written a single book. You are the very reason that we have dared to pursue our dreams. All your feedback, cheering comments and many questions help us improve our way of cooking every day.

Green Kitchen at Home by David Frenkiel and Luise Vindahl

First published in 2017 by Hardie Grant Books

Hardie Grant Books (UK)
52–54 Southwark Street
London SE1 1UN
hardiegrant.co.uk

Hardie Grant Books (Australia)
Ground Floor, Building 1
658 Church Street
Melbourne, VIC 3121
hardiegrant.com.au

British Library Cataloguing-in-Publication Data. A catalogue record
for this book is available from the British Library.

ISBN: 978-1-78488-084-2

Publisher: Kate Pollard
Senior Editor: Kajal Mistry
Editorial Assistant: Hannah Roberts
Publishing Assistant: Eila Purvis
Photographer: David Frenkiel
Design: Clare Skeats
Recipe Tester: Nicola Moores
Assistant: Sophie Mackinnon
Copy Editor: Laura Nickoll
Proofreader: Lorraine Jerram
Indexer: Cathy Heath
Colour Reproduction by p2d

Printed and bound in China by 1010

10 9 8 7 6 5 4 3 2 1